States of **BLISS**
& *yearning*

To
Murdo Ewan M^{ac}Donald
mentor,
preacher
and
mimic

States of **BLISS**
& *yearning*

The marks and means of authentic Christian spirituality

John L. Bell

First published 1998

ISBN 1 901557 07 3

Copyright © Wild Goose Resource Group

John L Bell has asserted his right
under the Copyright, Designs and Patents Act, 1988,
to be identified as the author of this work

Published by Wild Goose Publications

Unit 15, Six Harmony Row, Glasgow G51 3BA

Wild Goose Publications is the publishing division of the Iona Community.
Scottish Charity No. SC003794. Limited Company Reg. No. SCO96243.

All biblical quotations, except where otherwise specified, are from
The Revised English Bible © Oxford University Press and
Cambridge University Press 1989

Cover: © Graham Maule, 1998

Distributed in Australia and New Zealand by Willow Connection Pty Ltd,
Unit 7A, 3-9 Kenneth Road, Manly Vale NSW 2093.

Permission to reproduce any part of this work in Australia or New Zealand
should be sought from Willow Connection.

A catalogue record for this book is available from the British Library.

Printed by The Cromwell Press Ltd, Trowbridge, Wilts.

CONTENTS

Introduction

This is primarily and unashamedly a book of sermons.

Preaching and hymnody are my two terrestrial passions, largely because they are not solely for specialists but should affect the whole people of God.

Sadly, in the present climate, sermons suffer from a low profile within the Church. This may be indicative of a crisis of belief in this form of communication among those who have been ordained or appointed to preach the Gospel. Or it may be that boredom has masqueraded as pulpit piety and we have not named it.

While I am fully aware that there are other means by which people become informed of the Christian faith and have the Bible opened to them, I still regard preaching as a unique mode of communication when it becomes for preacher and congregation an experience rather than the flawless reading of a dissertation.

The careful reader will therefore note that there are changes of style from chapter to chapter. For this I make no apology.

The opening chapters originally constituted a lecture on spirituality given in a large canvas marquee. The sermons thereafter were delivered in a motley assortment of local churches, chapels, cathedrals and assembly halls. They are therefore neither homogeneous in type nor systematic in progression.

What is reflected is my belief that the people, the building, the text, the time of day and the subject matters should all inform the choice of vocabulary and style of delivery. Only thus can the eternal Word come close in the people's hearing.

Therefore, there has been little revision to the texts in the hope that the ear may hear the material all the while the eye reads it.

I acknowledge my indebtedness to congregations on both sides of the Atlantic whose invitation to preach and whose gift of their listening lie behind this book.

John L. Bell

June 1998

1 Dubious Beatitudes

The other morning I had a conversation with my newsagent.

He is Pakistani by birth, has lived in Britain for over 20 years and votes Scottish Nationalist.

We were discussing a trend in Britain which he finds distasteful – the intention of a minority of people to live off state benefits rather than seek work for which they are able. He commented approvingly on plans recently revealed by the government to get such people from welfare into work.

His conversation was not scandalous. He did not belittle people who had no possibility of working because of ill health or family commitments. His main criticism was directed at that selfish hedonism whereby people believe that they should get what they want and do what they like, irrespective of the cost their self indulgence demands of others.

We agreed on two things: firstly that life was not all about getting what we wanted or doing what we liked.

And then he, a Muslim, and I, a Christian, agreed that one of the purposes of the great world religions was to enable people to face up to what they would rather avoid.

The more I have mused on that, the more I am convinced that in the dominant hedonistic culture which is ours to adopt or transform, spirituality has precisely that high calling and function.

This is so because spirituality is not chiefly concerned with prolonging states of ecstasy, rapture or private religious intensity. When that is its primary function, then religion can rightly be accorded the Marxist accolade of 'opiate of the people'.

Spirituality is the oil which fuels the machinery by which we relate to God, to God's world and to God's people. It is a dynamic entity, not a static one. It pervades all of life and is not simply the preserve of special moments in sacred places.

We know this because whenever we look at the lives of biblical or national saints, the documentation of their religious experience is never one of a permanent high as if they were intravenously connected to a cannabis plant.

SPIRITUAL GIANTS

Moses is recognized as a person of deep spirituality not simply because he prized the prophetic ecstasy into which God threw fifty leaders and wished that all the people could be prophets.

He is regarded as a spiritual giant because he had to struggle with his past history of being a murderer, with his dubious identity as an Egyptian–sounding Jew, with his stammer.

And he had to struggle with recurrent aggression and antipathy from the very people he had delivered from slavery, a battle which forced him to shout at God regarding his 'charges',

> *Am I their mother?*
> *Have I brought them into this world*
> *and am I called to carry them in my arms*
> *like a nurse with a baby,*
> *to the land promised by you on oath to their fathers?*
> (Numbers 11.12)

David is seen as a person of deep spirituality not just because he won victory after victory for God from adolescence onwards, not just because he was anointed as God's chosen by Samuel, nor even because he had a prodigious talent for words and music.

He is regarded as a spiritual giant because, among other things, he had to cope with the incessant jealousy of his father–in–law. And he had to deal with the guilt of being a murderer and an adulterer, as well as with the grief of losing his firstborn.

And if we move into the New Testament, we will similarly find that the attestation of Paul's fitness to being a person of deep spirituality comes, of course, from his special visitation and calling as an apostle, his religious pedigree and his theological astuteness.

But it is also attributable to how he coped with his thorn in the flesh, a disputatious church at Corinth, and persecution by fellow Jews and Roman officialdom.

No one . . . no one . . . no one . . . who is regarded as a spiritual giant had it easy, did only what they wanted to do, got exactly what they liked.

Amen says Francis of Assisi, the impoverished one;

Amen says John of the Cross, the tormented one;

Amen says Columba of Iona, the exiled one;

Amen says Hildegaard of Bingen, the suspected one;

Amen says Julia of Norwich, the infirm one;

Amen says Martin Luther, the doubting one;

Amen says Teresa of Avila, the discouraged one;

Amen says Helder Camera, the controversial one;

Amen says Dorothee Solee, the disregarded one.

There is no authentic spirituality, there is no deep faith conviction, there is no true devotion which emanates from a life which is constantly pleasure–filled and pain–free. All the true saints of God never got what they wanted, did what they liked, or lived on cloud nine.

So when we, in our present cultural context, wish to define or distinguish the role and purpose of spirituality, it is not to legitimize escapism. It is to enable flaccid hedonists to face up to what they would rather avoid.

LISTS OF THE BLESSED

To legitimize our claim, let us look for a moment at two favoured repositories of Christian devotion. The first is the Book of Psalms.

Psalm 1 begins with the acclamation:

> *Blessed is the one who does not take the advice of the wicked as a guide.*

> Psalm 2: *Blessed are those whose refuge is the Lord.*

> Psalm 32: *Blessed are those whose God is the Lord.*

> Psalm 41: *Blessed is the one who is concerned for the helpless.*

> Psalm 61: *Blessed is the one you choose and bring into your courts.*

> Psalm 84: *Blessed is the one whose strength is the Lord.*

> Psalm 106: *Blessed are they who act justly.*

> Psalm 128: *Blessed is everyone who fears the Lord.*

One would imagine that with all this claim and promise of blessing about, life for the writers and for Jewish devotees in the 9th century BC would have been a bed of roses.

Why then should the same writers, the *same* writers, who claim that those who fear God and act justly are in a state of bliss, elsewhere write less memorable verses such as:

> *I am wearied with moaning,*
> *all night long my pillow is wet with tears.* (Psalm 6)

> *Rescue me from my pursuers*
> *before they tear at my throat like a lion.* (Psalm 7)

> *Why stand far off, O Lord,*
> *why hide away in times of trouble?* (Psalm 10)

> *My God, my God, why have you forsaken me?* (Psalm 22)

> *I kept completely silent, I refrained from speech;*
> *and my agony was quickened.* (Psalm 39)

> *You have made us a joke among the nations,*
> *you have exposed us to the contempt of our neighbours.*
> (Psalm 44)

> *Why should foreign nations ask,*
> *'Where is your God.'* (Psalm 79)

> *How can we sing the Lord's song*
> *in a foreign land?* (Psalm 137)

Is it that the psalms which proclaim the blessedness of God's servants were all written before hard times came?

No. There is no evidence to suggest that.

Is it that the psalms of blessing were written by optimists and the psalms of distress written by people who had a different rating on the Enneagram?

No. The same people wrote both.

Is it that the psalms of blessedness spoke from a condition of innocence, and the psalms of lament were the result of personal or national wickedness? No. Those texts which are sometimes referred to as *psalms of disorientation* were not simply concerned with guilt and sin. Not every shadow emotion – doubt, anger, regret, dismay – is necessarily nefarious.

What we have to conclude is that the *bane* was part of the *blessing*, that the misfortune was not the other side of the coin, but part of the same reality of living in the light of and under the jurisdiction of a benevolent God.

When we come to the gospels, Jesus makes manifest that this is true, though our familiarity with the Beatitudes might have numbed our mind to how their daring proclamation offends common sense.

Blessed . . . (and remember when Jesus says 'blessed' he is not indicating an eschatological or future state of completion. The blessing is known now.)

Blessed . . . are you who are poor!

Blessed are you who (*now*) go hungry!

Blessed are you who weep (*now*)!

Blessed are you when people hate you!

And if some object that here I am using the Lukan beatitudes for effect, then let's turn to Matthew to finish the octave:

Blessed are the gentle. (In the cut–throat economy?)

Blessed are those who forgive. (In the litigious society?)

Blessed are those whose hearts are pure. (When only the scandalous are given airtime?)

Blessed are those who make peace. (Even when they speak critically of the State of Israel, or question our economy's reliance on arms exports?)

Jesus was both more shrewd and more direct than David, Asaph and the other psalmists. He did not separate the weals and the woes into two separate categories. In his manifesto for human blessedness, in his people's charter for spiritual fulfilment, it is not only evident that the road to holiness leads through the world of action. It is also clear that those who wish to know the deep joy and consolation of faith will be required to experience other less attractive depths. And this because Christian faith is holistic. It embraces the totality of life in all its robustness and fragility.

Those who wish to know the bliss of shouting Hallelujah need also to know the yearning of those who cry 'How long?'

2 The Discipline of Remembering

If we wish to develop and be nourished by a spirituality which is holistic, and embraces both bliss and yearning, there are three strategies or disciplines we might do well to pursue. But when we think of the term 'discipline' let us not tarnish it with the negative connotations of restrictions on childhood behaviour. Rather we should see it as a term indicative of branches of learning, in the way that science or the arts are spoken of as 'disciplines'. While it may be our goal that 'prayer should be as natural as breathing', there are situations in which we have to learn how to inhale and exhale.

None of the disciplines or strategies is an instant answer to spiritual dilemmas. They are not pills to be popped, or blueprints for guaranteed success. They are exercises open to amendment, and – like the best lessons – they take time and rely on integrating theory and experience.

They are not esoteric, they are very straightforward. They are enshrined in the Psalms and in the Gospels, but they are vastly underrated and hence underused.

The first is *remembering*.

Many people of the older generations were reared on a musical diet of Redemption Songs, one of which had the refrain:

> *Count your blessings,*
> *Name them one by one*
> *And it will surprise you what the Lord has done.*

Because the tune never appealed to me, I disregarded the text for most of my life believing, in any case, that remembering was an activity which mainly occupied senior citizens in their dotage. This attitude is, in itself, a by-product of contemporary Western culture which tends to distrust the memory and breeds new generations of people who will only believe such data as is storable in photographs, diaries or word processors.

SELECTIVE MEMORY

Beware the age of information, because those who control it will also control human remembering.

Just as in Germany prior to, during and after the last war, there was an eradicating of information about the Jewish population to facilitate their proposed extermination, so other countries have ways of ensuring that the national memory is woefully selective.

In previous years, many who studied history at secondary school in Scotland left their alma mater in ignorance of sorry yet important periods of our national life such as the era known as the *Clearances*. This was an episode in the 19th century in which the nobility and their lackeys were involved in a process of forced expatriation of the inhabitants of the highlands and islands.

Crofters and their families were driven from their ancestral glens and either resettled on barren shorelines or exported, in their thousands, to the countries of the New World.

We were not encouraged to remember this era, because it was uncomfortable: uncomfortable to a nation which prided itself in civilizing the world; uncomfortable to lowlanders like myself whose ancestors were involved in this sin against humanity; uncomfortable to clergymen like myself whose predecessors, tempted by domestic and pecuniary advantage, gave their blessing to the involuntary mass transit.

It is a similar erasing or controlling of the corporate memory which has so annoyed so many Irish nationalists. In Gerry Adams's recent autobiography, as in the reflections of many of his compatriots, there is an expression of anger and regret that the history taught in the schools bore little relationship to what the Irish peoples had come through.

In the Jewish tradition, memory and remembering were essential to spiritual health. Thus the Passover ritual involved the asking of a question by the youngest male regarding the significance of the meal. To this the head of the household responded with a history of the origins of the feast which first rehearsed and later celebrated the deliverance of the Jews from slavery.

It is in remembering, in assiduous, careful remembering, that we may discover either that the past was much more exciting than the present or – equally important – that it was much worse.

And remembering is not meandering reminiscence.

If, rather than accurately calling to mind the events of the past, we casually speculate, invent or embroider, then sentimentality or subjectivity may assume the mantle of truth; and an imagined past, ultra-bloody or rosier than the sunset, will replace reality.

It was the result of selective and fevered reminiscing which Moses had to deal with at the doors of the promised land, where the very people whom he had led out of Egypt and through the wilderness refused to go forward into the future God had in store for them.

They hear and believe rumours that the territory ahead is overrun with giants who will annihilate them. And then they reminisce rather than remember. They who so recently were having their male children killed at birth, they who lived in a condition of exploitation and slavery, they who had to make bricks without straw, these very people begin not to remember but to reinvent history.

Moses has to counteract the majority of desert pilgrims who, rather than thank God for past deliverance and trust God for the future, raise their voices in the reactionary jibe:

> *'Back to Egypt!'* (Numbers 14.3)

There is a Back-to-Egypt brigade in every congregation, and there is a Back-to-Egypt corner in every soul, as in the face of the uncertainties ahead of us we retreat into selective reminiscing about the halcyon days which never really were. Such romanticizing, sentimentalizing, fantasizing about the past can only be displaced by true and honest remembering.

ACCURATE REMEMBERING

Sometimes, when I hear people in my own tradition bemoaning the present state of the Church and wanting to retreat to the good old days, I have to ask which good old days:

When women were always referred to in church by their husbands' Christian and family name – Mrs Matthew Grant, Mrs Alastair McGuinesss?

When pews could only be occupied if you had paid an annual seat rent?

When women who had been impregnated in whatever circumstances outside wedlock were publicly pilloried during divine service?

When sermons lasted for 40 minutes each (and sometimes there were two of them)?

When there was no heating, poor lighting, and spiritual means testing for those who wished to receive holy communion?

When the richest person in the community chose and controlled the pastor?

It is by accurate remembering that we gain a true perspective on the past, can gauge how far we have travelled, and recognize the blessings which may be counted.

But we also remember in order to restore our energy for the present.

This is the testimony of the psalmists, most appositely put in two poems, which come respectively from situations of personal and corporate despair:

Psalm 42   *As I pour out my soul in distress,*
             I call to mind
             how I marched in the ranks of the great to God's house,
             among enthusiastic shouts of praise,
             the excited noise of the pilgrims.

Psalm 137   *If I forget you, Jerusalem,*
             may my right hand wither away.
             If I forget you,
             may my tongue stick to the roof of my mouth.

Remembering the past not only puts the present in perspective. In the time of depression, of sadness, of persecution, of doubt, when everything seems desperate and we cannot see beyond our immediate circumstances, remembering the past may enable us to draw on emotional and spiritual energy to counteract the pessimism of our present situation.

STRENGTH FROM REMEMBERING

But that will only be true when the specific details of past deliverances, past surges of fervour, past moments of clarity, are accurately recounted.

Hence we dare, in the funeral parlour, remember that Jesus Christ rose from the dead. It does not remove sadness or become a substitute for grieving; it puts death in a context bigger than the grave.

Psalm 77 is an ideal example of how accurate remembering can provide the much needed energy to enable someone to cope with their present plight. Here, several verses are paraphrased, but the intention of the Hebrew text is carefully preserved:

> *Will God always reject me? Will he never respect me.*
> *Has God's love for me failed utterly?*
> *Has his grace been forgotten, has he grudged me compassion,*
> *does his right hand not strengthen or free?*
> *I refused to be comforted easily*
> *and the tears of distress made me blind.*
> *I turned faint when my thoughts went too deep for me,*
> *and I groaned when I called God to mind.*
>
> *Then at last I remembered all the things I'd forgotten,*
> *all the wonders you, Lord, had begun.*
> *And I saw how misfortune had distracted attention*
> *from the care constant in all you've done.*
> *Now I'm sure that your way is a holy way,*
> *for its progress and path I can see;*
> *and I know that your faithfulness in the past*
> *will be real and be present for me.*

When we come to the gospels we find Jesus constantly reminding his critics of portions of scripture or of historical realities which they have conveniently forgotten. But, most poignantly, we discover his investment in our memories when, during the last meal he shares with his disciples, he takes two elements of a larger feast, names them as symbolic of his sacrifice on the cross and says,

> *Whenever you do this,*
> *do it to remember me.*

And perhaps in that phrase, *Do it to remember me*, the meaning and significance of remembering are fully liberated.

Because, yes, we break bread and share wine to recall the history of the sacrament. And, yes, we break bread and share wine that the grace of God, which is bigger than our imagining, may transform our lives and ensure their place in the purposes of heaven.

But when we *remember* in the eucharist, we are also re-presenting to ourselves the reality of Christ's sacrifice. In Holy Communion we are present to the love of Jesus as through his chosen symbols he makes himself available to us. It helps if we realize that the alternative to *re-membering* is *dismembering*.

REMEMBER OR DISMEMBER?

When we remember, we put something together again with the possibility of reliving or re-presenting the experience. When we dismember, we fragment, break up the past, live out of abstracted notions of our history and our destiny.

And I would suggest that the culture of which we are part is one more interested in *dismembering* than *remembering*.

It seems keener to dismember families by targeting the volatility and clannishness of teenagers than to integrate them into all-age communities; keener to dismember innate abilities by proclaiming that every task needs specialist assistance than to affirm the wisdom and skill which many ordinary people carry within them; keener to dismember our engagement with reality by promoting virtual reality than to engage us with the non-fictional world which calls out to be cared for.

And the spiritual antidote which the Christian faith proclaims and offers is *re-membering*.

For through remembering, we are put in touch with our roots in all their radicality and vulnerability. Through remembering we bring to mind the forgotten potentials in our past on which we can still draw today. Through remembering we discover that any present dilemma is not disconnected from what has happened before, and that the God who saw us through past tragedies will see us through our present difficulties. Through remembering we take the broken or wrongly assembled jigsaw of our lives and discern our proper pattern.

But it takes time.

3 The Discipline of Waiting

Remembering takes time. Much more so does the second spiritual exercise or strategy. And it is very countercultural. It is anathema to the lifestyle which most of us espouse and encourage at work and at home.

It is the discipline of *waiting*.

Ours is an era which has prized and exalted the instant remedy, the instant answer, the instant fix. Anything which involves time, maturing, waiting before the results are discernible, is presumed to belong to a previous and more primitive era. I sometimes wonder what James Watt, inventor of the steam engine, or Alexander Graham Bell, inventor of the telephone, would say if they reappeared on earth today and were informed that their celebrated inventions were regarded not only as primitive but also as slow.

For today when we think of engines which enable transportation we think of jet planes and space rockets, not steaming boilers on traction vehicles. And today when we think of the communications industry, we think of surfing the web, linking up audio-visual conference calls, accessing in our spare room, via the Internet, more information than the British Library could store in print. We do not think of an electric wire conveying a crackling message from a person in one building to a person in another.

If we have a complaint about technology today, it is that we are unable to keep up with it. We are impatient to discover more; we resent having to wait.

At the risk of being labelled a technophobe, eccentric or Luddite, I want to ask whether we should necessarily encourage or compete in the race sponsored by information technology. Not denying the myriad advantages of the communications revolution, let us consider three realities.

INFINITE INFORMATION

The Internet offers to its users on tap almost infinite access to infinite information. New web sites appear daily enabling access to the minutiae of everything that is artistic, erotic, esoteric or educational, and much more.

However, despite having unlimited information on tap, we are in possession of bodies and brains which do not have the same infinite capacities. There is only a certain amount of information that we can assimilate, and there are a limited number of hours in the day in which we are awake and aware enough to do that.

If, as is allegedly the case, an increasing number of people spend an increasing number of hours in front of the Internet, this does not guarantee that the population will become better informed or more intelligent. The capacity to store or get information is one thing. It is entirely another to know what to do with that which you have acquired. We may have access to the innermost recesses of neolithic burial cairns courtesy of visual imaging which we can access in our bedroom. But, to use the language of the Authorized version, 'With all our getting, have we got wisdom?'

Years ago, when George MacLeod published his influential book *Only One Way Left,* he commented on how people in the modern age were faced with the great possibility of being able to address the world through a microphone, but did not know what to say.

In our present context we may have speedy access to all the information we could ever want, but do we know what to do with it, given our fascination with speed and our unwillingness to allow things to gestate?

One of the advantages of that more primitive form of communication, the book, is that one can put it down or throw it down, scribble notes in the margin, and underline or query words or phrases to be returned to when the text thus far has been mulled over and digested. Do our computers, which appear so similar to television screens, similarly allow for argument and pondering? Or, like the televisions they resemble, do they so command our eyes, ears, mind and posture that we endow them with a credibility they do not deserve?

FREE COMMUNICATION AT A COST

The expansion of use of the cellular phone continues unabated. Once the preserve of businessmen caught in traffic jams, the phone has now become both a fashion accessory and an ever-vigilant companion. There are even schools in the country where teachers are apprehensive about banning the instrument from classrooms, so adamant is the expectation of pupils that an important message might be sent at any moment.

I would ban such phones in classrooms as eagerly as I would on public transport. When I travel by train, as I frequently do, my ears are constantly besieged by bleeps, alarms and conversations on which I deliberately eavesdrop in the hope of discovering something significant. But it never happens.

> *Hello darling. Is that you?*
> *Yes, this is me.*
> *It's just to say that I got the train after all.*
> *Are the kids off to school yet?*
> *What are they wearing?*
> *Is Robert taking his clarinet today?*
> *Yes, it's not too busy,*
> *I have a compartment to myself.*

The only other person is a guy with long hair who looks like a
sixties' dropout.
OK darling, I'll see you tonight.
Oh, perhaps you might ring me in the afternoon and tell me
how you got on at the dentist.
Yes, I should be back around five.
But I'll ring you just in case.

Now, there are two issues which such eavesdropping raises in my mind. The first is who is paying for this expensive phone call? Not the businessman. For him it is free. But the poor suckers who are the customers of his firm, when they buy insurance, knitwear or whatever, will be paying for him and others of his rank to make inane and unnecessary phone calls.

The other issue is to do with how important the caller thinks he (for it is usually a he) is, that he must be on tap all the time, whether in the bathroom, driving along the motorway, or riding on the train. (I am, incidentally, always amused by how such devotees of mobile phones look and sound so earnest when using their designer toy in public, despite the trivial nature of their conversation.)

The issue here has to do with whether it is good or bad for our humanity to be – and expect others to be – instantly accessible. Can we honestly expect stress levels in upper and lower management to be reduced if people in such positions are constantly on tap? Is it not desirable that for some time in the day those who are busiest are left to order their own thoughts rather than to order or be ordered by others?

INSTANT ANSWERS TO COMPLEX QUESTIONS

And then there is e-mail, which I dislike more than the other two put together.

My experience is that if you are sent an e-mail and you don't reply, you get the same message a day later asking whether your terminal is broken. The presumption is that those who have e-mail facilities have nothing better to do all day than stand next to the infernal machine, keen to make an instant response to whatever appears.

There are some issues on which such a response is possible. If one is being asked to verify that the colour of paint required for office redecoration is magenta, a swift yes, no or other comment can be made.

But if the request requires careful thought, that is very different. If I am asked, for example, to make an assessment of a person's suitability for a job, or to write a short article on technology and religion, I might want to muse over the issue for a while. I might want to consult with colleagues. I might want to do a draft and sleep on it.

But if the expectation of the enquirer is that because an e-mail has been sent, an instantaneous response should be forthcoming, it may be that through buying into speed-crazed communication, I am preventing truth, accuracy and measured reflection from seeing daylight.

TIME TO KILL?

The three phenomena here alluded to have the dubious accolades of speeding up communication and killing time.

Time is killed in the case of the computer because it denies the necessity for critical assimilation of facts. Time is killed in the case of the mobile telephone because it denies space for introspection and solitude. Time is killed in the case of e-mail because it discourages the gestation process required for measured thought. And in the process speed becomes the *sine qua non* of modern living.

We don't build cathedrals the way they used to. In the Middle Ages, the person who laid the foundations would hope that his great grandson might finish the pinnacle on the tower. Now – as in the case of the Dome at Greenwich – a vast edifice is planned today and put up tomorrow. Only the judgement of the future will vindicate the claim of the proponents that this is a work of art, or the claim of the critics that it is a symbol of the rejection of craftsmanship in preference to short-term expediency.

The expectation of instant results goes all the way through our living. We expect every supermarket to have every commodity we require, and every bookshop every book we want *now*. And if we have to wait, there is something seriously amiss.

We expect any medication we buy to work instantly. It may have taken our body three weeks to get into the mess, but we want to feel a difference in three hours.

Earlier in the summer, a rather irate clergyman was asking me about the new hymnary the Church of Scotland has commissioned.

'How long will it take,' he asked.

'About six years,' I replied.

'Why can't you get it out sooner. We need it now! How come it takes six years?' he demanded.

'How come a baby takes nine months,' I responded. 'If your wife is pregnant do you go to ask the doctor to try and get things speeded up a bit?'

Indeed, pregnancy might be the only remaining universal symbol of how waiting time, appropriate time, *kairos* as opposed to *chronos* or clock time, is an important element in life.

WAITING TIME

But the Psalms are full of it, full of injunctions to honour that time which is appropriate,

> *Wait on the Lord.*
> *Wait patiently on God.*

And Jesus is fond of it . . .

waiting for three days between hearing the news of Lazarus's death and going to the grave,

waiting until the accusers had dispersed before forgiving the woman taken in adultery,

waiting to listen to a haemorrhaging woman's request, while Jairus was beside himself with fear for his daughter,

waiting, wasting time at a well with a woman who wasn't of his own race or class,

waiting for the right time in which to make his way towards Jerusalem,

waiting in the garden until the time of arrest and telling his disciples to watch and pray,

waiting for three days in the tomb before resurrecting into life.

Waiting is an important countercultural spiritual discipline. And it is that for a number of reasons:

1. In the first place, instant decisions, especially as they affect our life and the lives of others, are not always the best.

When a woman presents herself to her doctor worried because she has had a headache for three days, it would be preposterous for the doctor immediately to diagnose a brain tumour, although some of the symptoms might match. Rather the doctor would consider a range of options, and decide on a timescale whereby, if the pain continued, the simplest causes would be eliminated and more serious possibilities considered.

Similarly, if within a marriage there is an evident tension between husband and wife, only a fool would instantly recommend separation pending divorce. A good counsellor would encourage the couple to give time for the discovery and then the resolution of causes of conflict.

A quick-fix mentality might be sufficient when dealing with the exhaust pipe on an ageing car which is soon to be consigned to the scrap heap. But the human mind, the human body and human relationships are much less mechanistic. The remedy for their ills is not always apparent, but often requires time, patience and careful pondering.

2. Secondly, waiting allows for the development of relationships which would never mature if first impressions were the last word.

I have two close friends who are sculptors. As part of their courting ritual, they go round skips and collect bits of wood, broken typewriters, disused sinks, pieces of metal grating and other dubious *objets d'art.*

Their discoveries lie in the backyard or are shelved in some corner of the house, creating intrigue until months later some magnificent artefact emerges, made from the piles of junk. Then I realize why it had lain so long. They needed to get to know it better, to see its potential, to develop a relationship rather than rely on first impressions.

Much more so our human relationships and our relationship with God depend on there being time for familiarity to develop in which hidden potentials are revealed, and the off-putting first impressions give way to a deeper appreciation.

3. Thirdly, waiting is the prerequisite for real intimacy. In personal

relations, the beloved will not give away what is deep in herself or himself until time and familiarity have enabled trust to develop and intimacy to be safe.

We would not, on a first meeting with a stranger, reveal every facet of our past sorrow, or every deep hope for our personal future. And we would refrain from such conversation simply on the grounds that we had not known the other person long enough. Why then should we expect God to reveal to us what is deep, or imagine that by some quick-fix formula we can develop a lasting intimacy with our Maker?

We should remember this particularly when we read the Bible. If the Bible is really the word of God – rich, deep and ultimately true and converting – we should not expect it to surrender its deepest gifts and insight on a casual first reading.

4. Finally, waiting is a sign of love. Indeed it is perhaps the most clear indication of whether or not love is true.

You wait for the person you love. You wait for their arrival, for their answer, for their consent, for their gift.

If we expect a double-glazing salesman to come at 3.30 and he doesn't appear within half an hour of that time, we would not feel compelled to wait. We would feel free to move either because he had clearly broken his word and was to blame, or because we didn't want double glazing in the first place and only agreed to see him out of pity.

But if our mother or our brother whom we hadn't seen for years were returning from abroad, and expected to be at our home or at the airport at 4.30, we would wait till 4.30 the next day. And we would do this because we do not relate to our relatives as customers of a business venture, but as those who are bonded to us through love.

Waiting is both a test of love and a sign of love. The amount of time I am willing to wait is an indication of the priority the other person, or

God, has in my life.

All of our life is lived in the face of the clock. Less evidently, all of life is also lived in the face of the Kingdom of Heaven. In the first context, timed is gauged chronologically; in the other we have to develop a sensitivity to the will of God and to feel for what and when is appropriate.

To be governed solely by clock time is not merely to run the risk of working ourselves into a frazzle by being subservient to other people's deadlines and expectations. It is also to exempt ourselves from the much more costly but infinitely more fulfilling practice of waiting

on God,

on God's word,

with God's people,

for the right time.

4 The Discipline of Imagining

If *remembering* has something to do with the past, and *waiting* something to do with the present, the third spiritual exercise is geared more towards the future. But it is equally countercultural and, in some religious circles, strongly suspected.

I refer to that activity which is called *imagining*.

In the eyes of many Calvinists, imagination is something of a bogus gift, to be suspected more than protected.

Where the hallmark of faith is regarded as the ability to keep oneself spotless before the world, to be able to quote scripture, and to offer personal testimony of God's grace, talking about visions and dreams is regarded as dubious.

It can be a highly subjective activity, and perhaps apprehension arises because of the close association of the word *imagine* with the word *image* – something we are forbidden to make for ourselves according to the second commandment.

THE SUSPECTED IMAGINATION

The Reformed churches have traditionally put a low profile on the arts – musical, visual and literary.

Reformed Christians in Europe have worshipped in oblong box buildings painted the most anaemic colours and totally devoid of any ornamentation. Architecture, sculpture and interior design were scorned in an attempt to guarantee purity or freedom from distraction in the liturgical space.

In the presbyterian Church of Scotland, not only were organs and choirs disdained at the Reformation, but indigenous folk melody, the mainstay of Lutheran chorales, was excised from congregational song. In a further move towards a lean musical aesthetic, only metrical psalms of a 1650 translation were sung in the 17th & 18th centuries to an ever decreasing number of tunes.

This suspicion of creativity and of the fruit of the imagination has, in some nations, created an unhealthy distance between people of artistic merit and the Christian faith. It is indeed a barren creed which proclaims that God delights not in red or orange, but in clergy grey; that prose is better than poetry; that monologue is better than dialogue; that mental concepts are superior to physical illustrations; that dullness is somehow next to godliness.

Just as some churches in the past looked askance at the use of the imagination, so in our present cultural context individual creativity is both highly extolled and carefully undermined. Rather than be inventive, we are encouraged to take our pick from a range of presented options. Free choice substitutes for originality. But we don't always recognize it.

THE CREATIVE IMAGINATION

We want to go on holiday, so we visit a travel agent. Soon we are confronted with brochure after brochure telling us where adventure is, where the sun is, where the most popular resorts are, where the themeparks are, how convenient the airports are, and what the restaurants are like.

Then we play one venue against another and finally, with the help of the assistant, make a decision and feel as if we have come through a major ordeal.

Later on in the day we bump into someone who says that she and her friend went to the USA, taking only a Greyhound bus ticket, two changes of clothing and a list of cheap bed and breakfast establishments . . . and they had the time of their lives. And we mumble, 'Why didn't I think of that?'

The reason, of course, is that the activity in the travel agent's was an exercise in choosing between given alternatives, not a process involving our creativity and imagination.

A similar realization dawned on me recently when I wanted to buy a present for a colleague. I had decided on either a candlestick or a mirror. So I tramped round five department stores noticing that the range of mirrors and candles in each was remarkably similar to that in all the others.

Then I walked down a side street and saw a small craft shop which had a range of highly attractive domestic fitments made from driftwood, stones and flotsam. Throughout the shop were candle stands, each one different, some incorporating mirrors, each one unique, and all hand-crafted from materials washed up on the coast of Cornwall.

As I picked up a beautiful hand-made item and compared it to the tiresome mass-produced goods I had looked at before, I realized what the difference was. The commercial stores had simply gone through each other's catalogues to develop new lines. But here was something produced by the fertile imagination of a talented individual.

BIBLICAL IMAGINATION

I want to reclaim the imagination as a Christian resource and *imagining* as a spiritual exercise. I reclaim it as a Christian resource because if we are made in the image of God, then we are in the mould of a great imaginer, whose ingenuity is such that no two of us are the same, nor are two animals, nor are two trees, nor are two days.

States of **BLISS** & *yearning*

Cloning, the process by which an animate being can be genetically replicated, may be celebrated as a great scientific advance, but it can also be regarded as evidence of the Fall.

God wishes the world to be filled with variety. So every sunset, every landscape, every rock formation is different from all the others; and everything that flies, walks or swims differs from all others of the same species. Late in the day, humanity develops technology to do the opposite, to produce animate objects which are exactly the same and, should permission be granted, to replicate the uniqueness of individual human beings.

It is not standardization and conformity which bring new life to the tired earth, but the exercise of prophetic imagination, such as is evident throughout the Bible. It is not simply the dreams of Jacob and Joseph, it is the visions of Jeremiah and Isaiah which gave to weary folk both a theology of recovery and a visible image of what recovery meant.

Thus speaks Isaiah to people who were tired, and tired of being tired:

> *The eyes of the blind will be opened,*
> *and the ears of the deaf unstopped,*
> *the lame will leap like a deer*
> *and the dumb will shout aloud.* (Isaiah 35.5–6)

and elsewhere:

> *Arise, arise Jerusalem for your light has come.*
> *Though darkness covers the earth and thick darkness the*
> *nations,*
> *on you the Lord shines and over you his glory will appear;*
> *nations will journey towards your light*
> *and kings to your radiance.* (Isaiah 60.1–3)

38

Thus Jeremiah speaking to his exiled compatriots:

> *Come back, virgin Israel.*
> *Come back to your cities and towns.*
> *How long will you waver my wayward child?*
> *For the Lord has created a new thing in the earth:*
> *a woman will play a man's part.* (Jeremiah 31.21–22)

Thus through Hosea, God speaks of undeserved and all-forgiving love:

> *Go and bestow your love on a woman*
> *loved by another man, an adulteress;*
> *love her as I, the Lord, love the Israelites.*
> *although they resort to other gods.* (Hosea 3.1)

What is happening in these passages? The people of God, not through logic, not through long sermons, not through political analyses, but through dreams and visions are being given a glimpse of another reality to which they can aspire. It is not in the pay of the intellect, it is the gift of God and requires the exercise of the imagination.

And when Jesus appears on earth, is this not the same gift he uses with such great effect? For in one place he uses parables which draw on true life situations and become pictorial paradigms of the Kingdom of God. In another place he deftly handles a tricky situation – pointing to a little child to illustrate true greatness in the middle of a crowd of men intent on scoring philosophical and theological points.

Or look at how he persuades his doubting disciples of the reality of the resurrection, not by offering convincing arguments, but by eating a piece of fish for breakfast. Ghosts, after all, don't eat.

In Christ we see the prophetic and priestly imagination at its zenith, and if we would follow him, that faculty which is the birthright of all God's children must not be suspected.

THE TRANSFORMING IMAGINATION

I wonder whether in the USA black citizens would still be socially crippled had it not been for the courage and imagination of Martin Luther King, all of whose public oratory is peppered with visions and imagining:

> *I have a dream . . . that one day . . .*

I wonder whether in India disease would not have more severely ravaged the nation had not Gandhi in kindness and simplicity demonstrated elementary hygiene rather than lectured to the illiterate about it.

I wonder whether in many parts of the Western world those who are mentally incapacitated would not have remained for ever on the edges of society, had it not been for the French Canadian Catholic priest Jean Vanier, who dared to dream the impossible: that there could be little communities in which the disadvantaged and the over-advantaged might experiment in living together in mutual dependency.

Let us be clear – no reformation ever happened, no renewal ever took place, no pioneering evangelism ever succeeded because a committee of men meeting in a rectangular room came up with the right formula.

The Holy Spirit is not predictable. She is untidy, disordering at times, provocative and wistful. And the Spirit is given that the young may see visions and the old dream dreams. And this is not simply a corporate, a public, witness. *Imagining* is given for the enrichment of our private lives as well.

The depth of our prayer life and our closeness to God through reading the scriptures are not dependent on a sense of dull pedantic duty, suited best to the cerebrally endowed. God does not forsake the imagination of his people and take up residence only in their intellects.

The person who lights a candle as an aid to prayer and closes her eyes to visualize situations in the Bible can be every bit as devout as the priest who scours medieval breviaries and Greek lexicons. But, sadly, it is the latter devotee's model of personal spirituality which is more likely to be publicly approved.

As with remembering and waiting, imagining takes time. And this is countercultural to a clock-dominated, high-speed, standardized society. But it is not countercultural to God.

For God has all time in his hands, and if we are going to share eternity with him, here is the place and now is the time to start living by the standards of heaven.

5 Tricky Bits in the Bible

Readings: Romans 13.1–7; St Matthew 7.15–23

> *Not everyone who calls me, 'Lord,*
> *Lord,' will enter the kingdom of*
> *heaven, but only those who do the*
> *will of my Father.*
>
> MATTHEW 7.21

I suppose that having heard that text, there may be some people who are relieved to discover that I am not expounding Romans 13, the passage in which, among other things, Paul says that:

we are to submit to those in authority,

we have not to rebel, otherwise we will be justifiably punished,

we are to pay taxes without any complaint

. . . and all this because the government is in position by God's grace and intention.

If you feel relieved that I have chosen to speak from the Gospel, I must now reveal that the text from Matthew is a decoy.

THE AWKWARDNESS OF SCRIPTURE

I *do* really want to address this embarrassing, prickly, awkward passage about being obedient to the civil powers if for no other reason than that within this quinquennium it may be expected of the Scottish public that they will vote in at least four elections, as well as express opinions in referenda. Within the next five years we will have been asked to vote in regional, Scottish, United Kingdom and European elections. And should we discover that the political complexion of the dominant party in any of these is diametrically opposed to our own, we must have some scriptural guidance to sustain us.

Sometimes my friends in England ask why, when the government at Westminster was not of the same political hue as that favoured by the majority of Scots, there was no rioting.

Why was there no rioting? Surely because Scots are good Calvinists who take God's word seriously. That means that even if one hundred per cent of this nation were to vote Nationalist and the government in London were Liberal, Socialist or Tory, we still would not rebel, because according to St Paul, our mentor, the government is there by God's design and we have to submit to it!

Well, that's one interpretation.

Is all this stuff about obeying the government a prickly passage, an awkward text, a contentious biblical issue? Then let's change the chapter and look at something much less controversial.

What about homosexuality?

That word is never far from the moral conscience of the churches. A few years ago the Church of Scotland debated two reports on the issue to the satisfaction of nobody. Around the same time the Roman Catholic church published the new catechism in English which, with its censuring of homosexual activity, led to a Mass in Westminster Cathedral being disrupted by lesbian and gay activists.

Both denominations, in their thinking about the issue, cited another part of the letter to Romans where Paul rules out what he calls 'unnatural behaviour between men'.

So, on that biblical basis, should we spray-paint the Cistine chapel, given that it was decorated by a homosexual? Should we ban cathedral choirs from singing anything – words or music – written by Auden or Britten or Tippet because they expressed 'unnatural desires'? Should we require every Christian to eradicate from his or her record collection anything written by Tchaikovsky – *The 1812 Overture, Romeo and Juliet, The Nutcracker Suite*, the *Pathetique* – because the composer was gay?

No wonder people avoid reading or preaching from Romans! The one chapter limits sexual activity, the next prohibits political revolt. What else might we find to upset or confuse us?

But without going any further, it should be clear that what we are dealing with here is not just personal preferences or dislike of the shade of the government in power, or the sexual orientation of a proportion of humanity.

If it were just these issues in themselves, life would be simpler. But what we are dealing with here is the way in which we use and understand the word of God.

GUILT ON ALL SIDES

And at this point, my conservative evangelical friends will want to shout hurrah and to point out how there is far too much liberalism in the pulpit, and too many preachers expounding the bits of scripture which they favour and explaining away or avoiding completely those parts which they don't like.

And I have to sympathize with my conservative evangelical friends, because they are speaking the truth (although maybe not in love). Liberal Christians have too often tried to avoid or explain away the puzzling miracle stories, the notion of a geographical heaven, the bodily resurrection of Jesus, the moral imperatives from St Paul which don't tune in with secular lifestyles.

That is true, and that is not to their credit.

But I also have to listen to my liberal friends making similar protests against their evangelical accusers.

Because undoubtedly it is true that in Leviticus carnal relations are prohibited between people of the same sex. And on that basis, some would start a witch-hunt. But Leviticus also says that anyone who is going to be a priest must marry a virgin. Now it's a long time since I have been at an Anglican ordination, but I don't seem to remember that issue being raised in questions to the candidate.

It is true that in Corinthians and in Romans Paul protests against homosexual relations, but he also speaks passionately about how those with authority in the church have no right to exercise that authority if they can't control their children. But I have never found in the *Evangelical Times* an injunction to ordained readers to resign their ministry if their kids are telling them where to get off.

Being selective with scripture is not just a sin of one wing of the Church. Everybody tends to avoid that which is not comfortable. Any denomination will jump up and down to have a report on personal morality, but how many will be as enthusiastic about a report on the morality of church investments, the stock exchange, debt collecting and the futures market – all of which are addressed by the Holy Scriptures?

Many churches, from time to time, will have a study paper or a debate or print leaflets about the evils of alcohol. But whenever did a church decide to do an in-depth study of that activity which, more than others, is proscribed in the Levitical law, the Psalms, the Prophets, the Gospels, and the Pauline letters? I refer, of course, to the phenomenon of malicious gossip.

Of course, one of the difficulties which we encounter in today's literate society, in which all can have the Bible in their hands, is that there is so much in it with which to contend. It's a bit like the story of the

Anglican bishop who ensconced himself in a first class railway carriage and lit up a large cigar. After a while the guard came along and said, 'My Lord Bishop, there's a sign up there which says NO SMOKING.' 'Yes,' said the bishop, 'and there's a sign over there which says WEAR SPIRELLA CORSETS. I'm just making up my mind which one to obey!'

I want to look at this issue of how we use and regard the scriptures – whether we just attend to the bits which agree with our world view or whether we look at them all, Romans 13 included. And I'd like to suggest three things that might be of help when we deal with whatever at first seems so disagreeable.

WHAT WE DON'T WANT TO HEAR

The first is that perhaps in the word we don't want to look at or hear God is confronting us with something from which we are running away. And our faith will never grow and our life will never deepen until we take that word seriously.

Very occasionally, when marriages are celebrated in church, there may be a scripture reading from the Song of Songs. This seldom visited biblical book is an erotic poem that never mentions the name of God, yet appears between Ecclesiastes and Isaiah. To some it is an embarrassing sequence of verses which talk about how the bridegroom has thighs of alabaster and the bride has breasts like clusters of grapes.

Why is it that this book is avoided so often?

Is it, perhaps, because it says that sex is healthy, should be enjoyed, and was meant as such in God's purpose? And is it that a traditionally male and celibate priesthood has prevented that book from being widely read, because men don't normally talk about these things except in salacious conversations or dirty jokes?

Each of us may know other passages of scripture which we regard as awkward or unpalatable. And the first thing we have to ask, in honesty, is whether in these scriptures God is confronting us with what we should avoid no longer, but investigate and pursue.

WHAT WE NEED TO ARGUE WITH

The second possibility is that in the awkward passages we may be confronted with a word we need to argue with, debate, turn upside down, look at from a different angle and – in some cases – disagree with.

If we believe that the Bible really is the word of God, then one of the most disrespectful things we can do with it is swallow it hook, line and sinker. That is just as bad as treating it with mindless indifference.

When someone says something profound to you, you do not simply hear it and store it at the back of your mind. You savour it, you chew over it, you discuss it with yourself or others and thus indicate the value that word has for you.

There is nowhere in the history of God's dealings with humanity that people have found the word of God easy. Many of the prophets, on being told by God what they had to say to the people, suggested that God ask somebody else. And when Jesus, in person, walked the earth he was continually in dispute, in conversation, in argument with his disciples, the Pharisees and the Sadducees about what the scripture meant.

I believe that occasionally, through the scripture, God challenges us to a fight, to a wrestling contest similar to that which Jacob had at the brook called Jabbok, in which only by struggling with the word do we begin to understand its meaning. Or, after the wrestling, we may stand back and say honestly to God, 'I do not agree.'

And, of course, it may be that, like Jacob, we will wrestle with God, be allowed to win and then, like Jacob, discover that we walk away wounded.

I have spent too much time with people who have been perturbed by a verse of scripture to expect everyone to understand or agree with everything. I have talked with people who read how they must 'honour their father and mother'. But when I heard their story, when I heard exactly what they had endured from childhood, I had to say, 'If that were my father, I would not honour him . . . despite what it says in the Ten Commandments. And I would account to God for my decision on the day of judgement.'

I have sat too often with women aggrieved by the masculinity of some of the Scriptures to say they must accept everything unquestioningly. Thank God that women do now argue with lines in Leviticus and verses in Paul's letters which seem to subjugate, diminish and deny them their full humanity and their full Christian potential.

God is not some celestial sadist whose chief delight is in watching biblical texts befuddle, debilitate and demoralize those made in the divine image. Maybe there are some texts which we shall just have to disagree with until the day of judgement and then see whether Paul or we were right. But until then we should not avoid them; we should argue with them, search for their significance or the deeper intention hidden behind the words.

THE WORD AND THE WORD

We have a third option when we are dealing with a tricky bit in the Bible, and that is to refer the word of God to the Word of God, to the one who became incarnate in order that light might be shed on our darkness.

As the Pharisees and the Sadducees discovered, one of the perpetually annoying features of Jesus was that he took texts which confused people and began to interpret in a new way. And he does that still.

Because of this, I end with the words with which I began:

> *Not everyone who calls me 'Lord, Lord,'*
> *will enter the kingdom of heaven,*
> *but only those who do the will of my Father.*

It is in association with these words that I want to look at the prickly passage of Romans 13.

If we take Romans 13 seriously as regards obedience to the state, then no Christian has the right to be glad about the downfall of apartheid in South Africa. Rather, we should denounce Desmond Tutu, Frank Chicane and Alan Boesak, all of them Christians, for being subversives and traitors.

For was it not biblically proscribed activity they indulged in when, in circumspect ways, they encouraged disinvestment in South Africa and boycotting of their nation's exports, measures which could only lead to economic ruin? Were they not going against good Pauline teaching when they encouraged people to stop paying for rent and fuel in the townships, and when they organized mass demonstrations against the elected government?

It was Boesak, himself a Calvinist scholar, who spoke in Edinburgh several years ago about how he viewed Romans 13, which seemed to condemn the activities of blacks who resisted the authorities. He pointed out how white South Africa regarded itself constitutionally as a Christian country. It was a country which said, 'Lord, Lord.' But it was also a country which clearly did not do the will of God. It was a country which denied and defiled the image of God in its black and coloured inhabitants. It was a country which imposed gruelling labour conditions on migrant workers, fleeced the poor of their limited finances, and paid indecent wages.

To support such a government was to encourage heresy. There was only one course of action for the Christian – to oppose the state. And in doing so, it was the word of Jesus which shed light on the words of Paul.

When dealing with the hard word in scripture, we may be confronting something that we should no longer avoid; we may be confronting that with which we should wrestle. Or we may have to seek illumination from the lips of Christ.

Whatever the situation, be assured that God allows us to converse, to argue, even to disagree with the word. Because God calls us into a *dynamic* not a static relationship with him. And in a dynamic relationship sometimes there are moments of supreme and absolute agreement. And sometimes there are moments of misunderstanding and argument. These are signs that the relationship is alive and not dead. These are signs that it is grounded in love.

6   A Changing God
or A Changing People?

Readings: Jonah 3.1 – 4.1; 2 Timothy 3.10–17

> *God did not inflict on the people of*
> *Nineveh the punishment he had*
> *threatened. This greatly displeased*
> *Jonah.*
>
> *JONAH 3.10 / 4.1*

THE CHURCH OF THE WORD

This is a Reformed Church, a Presbyterian Church, a Church – so its history informs us – which is built on the word of God; a Church whose elders and ministers are required to vow publicly that they hold the Bible to be the supreme rule of life and faith; a Church in which – at least in a previous era – a fair number of children would be required to memorize such texts as:

> *All scripture is given by inspiration of God, and is profitable*
> *for doctrine, for reproof, for correction, for instruction in*
> *righteousness.* (2 Timothy 3.16)

So, being a traditionalist, and calling on this proud Presbyterian legacy of putting the Bible at the centre, can I ask how we might have felt if the Old Testament reading had not come from Jonah, but from the book of Joshua? How would we have felt if I had read from Chapter 11 of that book? It recounts the attempts of the Israelites to settle in the promised land where innocent people were happily going about their business, until . . .

> *It was the Lord's purpose that the natives should offer*

> *resistance to the Israelites, and thus be annihilated, and*
> *utterly destroyed, as the Lord had commanded Moses.*
> (Joshua 11.20)

Or supposing we had read from Judges, just the first chapter . . .

> *The Lord delivered the Canaanites and the Perizzites into*
> *their hands, so that they slaughtered ten thousand of them.*
> (Judges 1.4)

Or perhaps something a little less bloody. What about a reading regarding that peace-loving man, King David, who wrote the Twenty-third Psalm and danced in public. Here we have David's exploits recounted in the second book of Samuel:

> *David made a great name for himself by the slaughter of*
> *eighteen thousand Edomites in the Valley of Salt.*
> (2 Samuel 8.13)

Shall I go on?

How would we have felt if one of these or many other similar passages had been read to us from the word of God which is the supreme rule of life and faith?

That's the kind of issue which critics raise, isn't it? That's the kind of evidence to which those who object to Christianity point when they claim that so many wars have been started in the name of religion and no wonder, because the Bible is full of stories about people getting killed in God's name by those God chose.

Have we not heard the accusations? And how do we reply?

RESPONDING TO REAL ACCUSATIONS

Do we say that Protestants don't actually believe everything that's written in the Bible . . . and fly in the face of archaeological evidence which proves that such battles did take place. Do we claim that not every part of the Bible carries the same weight, and then get accused of espousing that kind of 'pick and mix religion' more commonly associated with New Age enthusiasts?

Or do we say that the New Testament does away with the Old, and then have to face Jesus who says quite clearly, 'Oh no it doesn't,' and Paul who, knowing the Old Testament thoroughly, still claims that all scripture, *all scripture*, is profitable?

I have pondered this recently, out of a growing conviction that the bits of the Bible we would rather avoid might just be the ones we should attend to. And this either because our credibility as the People of the Book depends on our grappling with such thorny issues or, more pertinently, because it may be that, in the bits we avoid, God may be saying a word to us that we don't want to hear.

So, how do we deal with the gore and the blood and the killings which lie behind or beside praise songs in the Psalms and hopeful prophecies in Isaiah?

I want to suggest that there are two ways of dealing with this kind of material; and each has a price tag attached.

THE GOD WHO CHANGES

The first, which will disturb if not shock some people, is to suggest that the Bible is a record of God changing his mind about us.

That will upset those who believe that God *never* changes his mind, that the supreme property of the Almighty is to be absolutely changeless; that God has no new thoughts, no new attitudes; that what God believed on the first day of creation is exactly the same as what God will believe on the last day of eternity.

Now I don't doubt that God's love and mercy are unchanging in their intention and intensity. But I don't believe that this precludes God from changing his mind. Indeed, I believe that the Bible is the record of God changing his mind with regard to human beings.

It is the record of how God changes his mind as to who will be the beneficiaries of his love, thereby gradually widening the circle of God's friends. And I can point to precise passages in Holy Scripture where that is explicit.

After God floods the world and destroys all living creatures except for one small family, God says *'Never again will I destroy the earth.'* . . . It is as if God is having his compassion stretched from a few people to many.

Turn to the prophecy of Hosea, where God's heart is broken because people have been unfaithful to him, and in a most poignant moment, after threatening hellfire and damnation, God says:

> *How can I hand you over?*
> *How can I destroy you?*
> *A change of heart moves me,*
> *Tenderness kindles inside me.* (Hosea 11.9)

Or look, as we did earlier, at the prophecy of Jonah, where God has inspired the prophet to tell the people of Nineveh that their number is up. And when they change their ways, does God cynically sneer at their eleventh-hour conversion?

No, God changes his mind. The passage we read states:

*God relented and did not inflict on them the punishment he
had threatened.* (Jonah 3.10)

All the time, it seems, God's compassion, God's love, is moving in
ever-widening circles. At one time God loved one family and destroyed
all other families. Then he loved one tribe and destroyed all other
tribes. Then he loved one nation and destroyed all other nations.

And then . . . when God came in the flesh in Jesus, he loved the mul-
titudes, no matter whether they were his 'chosen' people or abject
heathens. That's what the feeding of the five thousand is all about.
That's what the healing of non-Jewish people is about. Can we feel
for that?

Can we feel for how, as God looks at more and more people, God doesn't
become more and more impersonal, distant, dismissive. As God comes
into contact with more and more people, his love changes focus from
being narrowly directed to an individual, a sect, until it embraces
those – even those – who don't know God's name.

Now if this is true – if the Bible is the account of God changing his
mind about us – there's a price tag. And we might not want to pay it.
It is simply that if we are made in God's image, that same ability to
change our mind and to widen the circle of our love should be evident in
us.

But such a possibility is not encouraged by the climate in which we
live, which puts the spotlight on individuals and disclaims responsi-
bility for corporate misfortune. It was well illustrated on the front
page of *The Observer* recently. The banner heading read:

> *A lone yachtsman is pulled from the ocean. The world gasps.*
> *Hundreds of immigrants disappear in the Mediterranean.*
> *Was it murder? Who even cares?*

> (© *OBSERVER, 12 JAN 1997*)

Take any story of the plight of an individual whose expensive regime of medical treatment is threatened by shortage of funds. Plenty of personalized emotion is encouraged there. Contrast that private dilemma with the plight of not one but tens of thousands of children in Cambodia, Mozambique and Angola who are the victims of land-mines, many of them made in Britain.

As reported in *The Guardian* recently, more than two thousand people are killed by land-mines every month. Most of them are civilians and nearly twenty per cent are 15 years old or younger.

Can we make the leap from feeling misty-eyed and moved by the plight of one person to being concerned about tens of thousands of children maimed by the products of our arms industries?

More pertinently, when it comes to an election, will we cast our vote depending on whether parties of the left and right promise to do good to *our* family and *our* pocket through lower taxation? Or will our sympathies widen to see taxation not as a curse but as a privilege which enables the elderly, the vulnerable, the sick, the unemployed, the homeless to be better cared for and integrated into society?

The Bible records the focus of God's love changing from being concentrated on one family, on one tribe and damn the rest, to becoming an all-embracing concern for humanity.

In this light, we can see the bloodshed and the battles of Joshua and Judges in a different context. But the price tag for that is that just as God's compassion, God's sympathy, God's love, broadens from the individual out, so must ours.

THE PEOPLE WHO CHANGE

But I said there were two ways of dealing with our dilemma of having a Bible peppered with divinely inspired violence.

The first is to see it as God gradually changing his mind about humanity; the second is to see it as humanity gradually discovering the truth about God.

We may regard the Old Testament not as flawed or wrong but as the record of people whose understanding of God was partial and at times deficient. They begin by believing that God is always on their side, so they kill anyone who is different.

Later, when they become aware that they can be every bit as malicious, bloody and unfaithful as their enemies, prophets like Jeremiah help to convince them that God is not always on their side, indeed that God is sometimes on the side of their enemies. Upsetting as that may be, it ensures that their picture of God becomes bigger and fuller. And no doubt, God will be behind this gradual development of their understanding of their Maker.

In much the same way, as children we had limited knowledge of our parents. They may have been perfectly honest with us, but they would not disclose everything until the appropriate age, stage, circumstances or questions allowed us to learn more. Indeed for some of us it was not until we left home for a while and came back, that we realized how adult and interesting our parents were!

So we may see a gradual development of people's understanding of God, a gradual changing and enlarging of their picture of God until, in the fullness of time, God comes in Jesus, and the whole picture is on display.

But if this is the case – if it is true that the Bible records the changes in human understanding about God – there's a price tag on that too.

And it's not one that many people want to pay. It's certainly not what Jonah wanted to pay. That's why he got angry with God. Jonah had a clear picture of what God was about. He believed that God was on the side of the religious establishment which he, as a prophet, embodied. Jonah had his theology right.

And suddenly, when God decided not to destroy Nineveh, but to pity the people, Jonah became upset. Because if this is how God really was, then Jonah would have to change his mind, swap his Sunday School certainties for something quite different. And he did not want to pay that price, so he went away to sulk.

We may empathize with him. We all tend to think that we know what God is like. And we have either grown comfortable with our understanding, or we have hated God because of it.

Two weeks ago I met a man in his thirties who had been an atheist for most of his life. He had been both the beneficiary and the victim of Scottish religious education. As a little boy, he had been taught hymns such as

> *God is always near me,*
> *Hearing what I say,*
> *Knowing all my thoughts and deeds*
> *All my work and play.*

As a child he had developed an understanding of God as some kind of celestial snoop who was obsessed with sins, who never smiled, and who hated those who didn't go to church. This young man would have lived with that impression until he died, had he not opened a Bible one day, and discovered other pictures of God, changed his mind and become a Christian.

But it is not just those who are outside the Church living off defective childhood images of God who have to change their mind; it's all of us.

God is bigger than the cosmic sadist who took our dearly loved granny away when we were ten. God is bigger than the old man in the sky who is obsessed with sexual conduct, but has no interest in financial misdemeanours. God is bigger than the Protestant deity who blesses the orange sash and despises the rosary. God has moved on from the hymns we sang in childhood. God has moved on from our conversion experience in the Kelvin Hall. God has moved on from the 16th-century language of the Authorized Version. God has moved on from the male-dominated assemblies that our churches used to be.

And the price to be paid for worshipping such a God is that our idea of God has always to be changing, always growing bigger.

So, where do you stand as regards the awkward bits in the Bible, the killings of innocent people, the genocide in God's name? Are these the beginning of the record of how God gradually changes his mind about humanity? Or are they the beginning of the record of how humanity gradually changes its understanding of God?

The price for believing the first is that our human sympathies, like God's, have to go beyond individuals to crowds, out of the personal into the political.

The price tag for the second is that our understanding of God has constantly to grow, to change, to be renewed.

Which one do you go for?

Or is there indeed a choice?

7 Against the Monoculture

Readings: Genesis 11.1–9; St Matthew 15.21–28

*The Lord came down to see the tower
and the city they had built
and God said, 'Here they are; one
people with a single language. Since
they have started to do this, from
now on nothing they have a mind to
do will be beyond their reach.'*
GENESIS 11.5

If you listened carefully to the two scripture readings, you might have been surprised at the selection.

From the Old Testament passage from Genesis Chapter 11, we read the story about the Tower of Babel which suggests that God does not approve of skyscraper architects.

And in the New Testament, in Matthew Chapter 15, we read the story of how Jesus – highly uncharacteristically – referred to a woman as a dog.

Surely there are easier stories!

Well, I suppose there are, so let me tell you about Wednesday night.

SURPRISE VISITORS

I had been advised by my secretary on Tuesday that two unidentified Americans were making their way round Scotland. They had phoned my office to say that they would be in Glasgow on Wednesday evening and, in tones which intimated we were the best of friends, suggested that they might take me out for a meal.

Never being one to look an American gift horse in the mouth, I waited with bated breath. Just as I was about to give up hope and start raking through the fridge for leftovers, at 6.30 p.m. precisely the phone went.

The voice said, 'It's Phil Conroy and Joe Wisinski.' (I was none the wiser.) 'Did you get our message?'

I said yes and they then informed me that they had just arrived in Glasgow from the north, would be travelling on to London on the overnight bus, wondered if they could take me out for a meal, and asked if I knew where they could leave their luggage. So I told them to get into a taxi and come to Kelvinbridge, where I live, it being only four minutes from the bus station; and I said that I would go out into the street to meet them.

In due course a taxi drove up and from inside it two pairs of hands beckoned me to come to the door. As I did, a large student jumped out, grabbed me, said it was great to meet again and . . . 'Is there any chance we could borrow some money. We only have dollars!'

My heart sank. I had seen this behaviour before – representatives of the self- confessed greatest nation in the world, believing that American currency should be valid everywhere.

I had seen it in the bookshop on Iona where wealthy Texans sometimes express not just astonishment but annoyance that the prices for everything are in pounds sterling, and then insist that the sales attendant translates the price into American currency. I had seen it when I worked in Amsterdam where, in a city which has some of the most exotic coffee houses and snack-bars in Europe, our transatlantic neighbours hunger and thirst until they find a MacDonalds.

And lest this seem like a tirade against Americans, the selfsame behaviour will be gloriously evident during the Glasgow Fair fortnight on the Costa Brava, as natives of the Dear Green Place presume that every Spanish waiter will understand their deepest desire for a 'fish supper'.

Now what has this to do with the tower of Babel . . . or the Syro-Phoenician woman? Nothing? Or everything?

It strikes me on revisiting this story of the Tower of Babel, after many years abstention, that like many of the awkward and disconcerting stories in the Old Testament, it speaks of something not obscure but relevant. To use technical language, it is a divine indictment against the monoculture. In plain speaking, it indicates that God intended diversity and not uniformity to be the pattern of our existence.

THE LURE OF THE MONOCULTURE

The people who built the Tower of Babel had only one language, and their sole purpose was to prove to themselves and to anyone else watching how superior they were. They did this by trying to demonstrate that big was best, building a monument to their own conceit to prove the point. And God would not tolerate it.

When any building, any enterprise, becomes an all-consuming passion, it displaces God and with God all those whom God shelters – the poor, the weak, the marginalized.

In this light, we may see the history of civilization as a story of rival nations struggling to become global powers and enforcing uniformity on the world. The British did that by colouring pink as much of the map as was possible, requiring English to be the lingua franca, and expecting people who knew nothing of London nevertheless to vow unswerving obedience to a monarch resident in that city.

In the process of building the Empire, Indians were transported to work in Central Africa, and West Coast Africans were transported in shackles and by the millions to become slaves on the eastern seaboard of the New World.

A contemporary example of the same phenomenon may be seen as the World Bank and the International Monetary Fund (both misnomers given that they are controlled by the West!) commend and impose Northern patterns of economic development unsuited to Southern-hemisphere nations. Hence the impoverished nation of Uganda, a former British colony, spends 4 per cent of its income on education, 3 per cent on health and over 14 per cent on paying back interest on loans from the North.

Similar patterns of imposed uniformity can be seen in the boasts of the mighty fast food chains that all over the world billions of their products are eaten every day. The cost to the earth which such proud empires exact, in their requirement that Central American forest lands be denuded of trees in order that beef cattle may safely graze, has yet to be properly calculated.

The Babylonian tower phenomenon was also evident in Scotland in the 60s and 70s when locally owned manufacturing industries were bought up by multinational companies which, before long, transferred production to cheaper parts of the globe and put thousands of workers on the dole. This was certainly the case in my own native town when eight major industries changed hands in almost as many years.

Oh, how I wish that then I hadn't kept the Bible so apart from my life that it did not inform it! Oh, how I wish that then I had seen in this odd story of the Tower of Babel God's adamant opposition to proud empires and enterprises whose primary goal is self-aggrandizement, never mind the cost or casualties in the wake.

We are not destined to be a monoculture, to be uniform. The differences that exist among nations and cultures, that make other people hard to understand or attractive, are there by divine design.

So, if you should happen to end up on the Costa Brava and no waiter can fulfil your need for a fish supper or hot-pea special, then thank God. And if you should end up in Rome and find it odd to be buying a cup of tea with lire rather than pounds sterling, thank God. And if you go into the West End of Glasgow and see second and third generation Pakistani or Indian restaurateurs offering a range of curries which no cholesterol-saturated white Glaswegian could ever make, then thank God for this glorious diversity.

And if, when you think of the Church, you imagine that ecumenism means that everyone will have a morning service just like ours, pray to God to protect us from such debilitating boredom.

THE GIFT OF DIVERSITY

I suppose I am luckier than most. My work requires me to be in different religious environments every week. Thus, last weekend I was in an Anglican Cathedral at 9.30 in the evening, where a choir of twelve men were singing compline from the back of the building. Half of it was in Latin, all of it was unaccompanied, and the building was packed with eight hundred people, the average age of whom would be twenty-four.

The previous evening I had been at worship in a Reformed Church in Olympia, Washington, where Presbyterians and Congregationalists were breaking out of their straitjackets in a service led completely by lay people, with everyone sitting in the round. And because many of the people who come to that service are needy, it was so designed that even a paraplegic girl who could scarcely speak was able to lead part of the worship.

And I think of the Sunday before that in a black Catholic parish, with the choir dancing up the aisles, the song of the people full-throated, the congregation spontaneously whooping and clapping, as the mass enabled both deep solemnity and deeper joy.

Who would ever want to obliterate these glorious differences in order that we had one perfect church with one anaemic catch-all liturgy?

The purpose of God in creation is not to make us all the same, and certainly not to allow political, economic or ecclesiastical empires to build monuments to their own pride irrespective of who is hurt. The purpose of God in creation and in history is to bring into being a world of glorious diversity which is held together in Jesus Christ.

And this is where the Syro-Phoenician woman comes in.

She appears at a point in Jesus' ministry where he is being recognized as the Messiah, the Jewish saviour, the hope of his nation, the fulfilment of Jewish prophecy. This woman who has a sick girl is not of Jesus' tribe or nation. Worse than that, her kind were so despised that a person of her race would be called a dog or a bitch depending on the gender.

Jesus is in the middle of his hand-picked Jewish disciples who want to keep him to themselves and only want people like them to have his attention. So up comes this woman and asks for help.

And he says, 'Listen, you don't take the children's food and throw it to the dogs.'

'Hurray!' cry James and John. 'Good for Jesus. Tell it like it is! Call a spade a spade, and don't mince your words.'

But there is, perhaps, a twinkle in Jesus' eye – enough to let the woman know that he is using that foul, racist language so she can challenge it.

She replies: 'It's true sir. You don't throw the children's bread to the dogs. But the dogs eat what falls from the children's table.'

And he looks at her, and he smiles at her, and he admires her.

And to the disgust of the disciples, he makes it clear that the grace of God, the love of God, the healing power of God, is not just for people who are like them.

God is not racist, separatist, elitist. God does not want everyone to be the same. The kingdom of God is not a monoculture.

'Go,' says Jesus, 'and because of your faith . . . (your non-Jewish faith, your unconventional faith in me) . . . because of your faith, your daughter has been cured.'

Here is God's great purpose – not that the world should become the same, but that the differences, the opposites, the unlikes, the awkward and antagonizing folk, should be healed and held together in Jesus Christ our Lord.

8   A Word in Public

Readings: Exodus 20.1–18; Philippians 3.4–11

> *And God spake all these words*
> *saying, 'I am the Lord thy God*
> *which have brought thee out of the*
> *land of Egypt, out of the house of*
> *bondage.'*
>
> *(EXODUS 20.1)*

Many people might not only recognize these words, but be able to repeat them and the seventeen verses of Exodus Chapter 20 that follow.

A GOOD OLD SCOTTISH CUSTOM

The Ten Commandments was, until relatively recently, a text which was often committed to memory in Scottish primary schools, forever to swim around in the subconscious of former beneficiaries of Scottish education along with the twelve times table; the information that 'a verb is a doing word' while 'an adverb modifies a verb, adjective or other adverb'; and the odd poetry stanza beginning,

> *'I will arise and go now, and go to Innisfree'*

or   *'I wandered lonely as a cloud that floats on high'*

or   *'Slowly, silently, now the moon'*

or   *'Wee sleekit, cowrin', tim'rous beastie'*

The memorizing of the Ten Commandments was common practice not just because, in the King James Version, the text was good poetry. Rather, along with the Lord's Prayer and the Beatitudes, this text was considered to be one of the key scriptural passages on which life and faith should be based.

And, like the Lord's Prayer and the Beatitudes, and even the Apostles' Creed, there was a fashion in Presbyterian churches in Scotland, as in Reformed church buildings on the continent, to have the Decalogue (for that is also its name) painted on the walls, or on the ceiling, or on a large board which could appear in the sanctuary or the schoolroom.

And even yet, even when schools no longer encourage children to exercise their memory with regard to religious texts; even today when churches have substituted fashionable banners for forbidding scriptures as a form of mural decoration; even today when the vast majority of the British public does not subscribe to the liturgical practices as offered by the historical denominations; even today, an appeal to base life and behaviour on the Ten Commandments will resonate in the national psyche.

What a hold this ancient Jewish text, once written in tablets of stone, has three thousand years after its initial reception on Mount Sinai!

STERN LAWS OR LOVING WORDS?

Yet I would venture to suggest that what exactly the Ten Commandments constitute may be a mystery, albeit a manageable mystery, to the great British Public. It's a bit like *The Financial Times* or the Dow Jones Share Index or the Isobar Chart – terms which greet us nightly on the 6 o'clock news, but may be fully comprehended by only a minority.

Some people, maybe even most, regard the Ten Commandments as a set of laws. Some, maybe also most, consider them as primarily concerned with personal morality. Others yet may believe that they are the means by which God tries to guarantee good behaviour.

I shall not say that nothing could be further from the truth. But I will say that such opinions fail to grasp the full significance of the Ten

Commandments. They are not primarily an indication of God wanting people to behave properly. God may be judge of all the earth, but that is not God's only role.

Walter Brueggeman, one of the most incisive and lucid of contemporary biblical scholars, argues forcibly that the Ten Commandments were not given by some kind of censorious deity made in the image of Calvin or Knox at their dourest. Rather, he sees the Ten Commandments as the means by which God shows deep compassion for his people.

Knowing that endless work is bad for the body and for the soul, and knowing how his people suffered in Egypt under a punitive regime, he decrees that six days are enough. God has heard the cry of the exploited, and in the Sabbath commandment he responds positively to their need.

By extension, we might see how the commandment not to commit adultery was not simply a matter of God trying to bridle the unruly libidos of Jewish males, but was also a way of safeguarding women, who had low standing in Jewish society. It was a response to the cries of those who had been abused, cheated, wasted.

And as for not bearing false witness – lying against, slandering, your neighbour – what is that if not a compassionate response to the cries of those who, having no money, having no influence, could be misrepresented without fear of challenge or prosecution?

Indeed the titles Decalogue or Ten Commandments, the Latin and English terminology for this renowned section of Exodus 20, are misnomers inasmuch as the ancient Jews never used such legalistic terminology. They called them the Ten Words, seeing them as the gracious and providential statements of a God who cared before he condemned. That is why, throughout the book of Psalms, we find recurrent phrases which may seem alien to us, about how the writer 'loves' the commandments of God.

Far from being the restrictive legislation of a celestial bully, the Ten Commandments are words of grace and care given to humankind by a God who responds to the cries of those who have been wronged.

But more than this – and certainly at variance with popular opinion – the Ten Commandments were never initially regarded as being rules for personal behaviour, legislation for private morality. These words were addressed to the whole community, and the whole community assented to keep them. Thus the German biblical scholar Gerhard von Rad writes

> *The* 'Thou shalt' *form of address is directed to Israel (the nation), as well as the individual. It is the form of address . . . belonging to a time when the individual standing in independence over against a group is still unknown.'*
> (*Old Testament Theology* Bk 1, © Oliver Boyd Ltd. 1962)

Here, then, we have a prescription for living which is intended to have an effect not simply on private behaviour, personal morality. It is a word addressed to communities and to society. This makes the Ten Commandments much more penetrating and relevant than many of their proponents imagine.

THE TEN FOR TODAY

For when addressed to the nation, what must be the response to such words as: 'Thou shalt have no other gods before me?'

Unlike the ancients, unlike the Greeks and Romans, we don't have idols, we don't carve huge statues of Mars, the god of war. We just have an armaments industry which, with its French and American counterparts, is responsible for the production of 60 million land-mines peppered all over the southern hemisphere which maim and kill innocent children in places like Mozambique and Angola.

We don't make effigies of Eros and Aphrodite, the god and goddess of carnal pleasure. We just have tabloid newspapers which elevate to the status of celebrity those whose sexual predilections are excessive or freakish, while at the same time trying to cripple by smear and innuendo genuine celebrities who espouse lives of modesty.

We don't have a cult worshipping Fortuna, the goddess of luck. Instead we have a nation of would-be millionaires who queue up on a Saturday to play the lottery, blindly assenting to what is tantamount to a tax on the poor, the revenues of which will furnish the pleasure domes of the wealthy.

How, if it is a corporate word of grace, does a community or nation respond to the injunction not to steal? As long as that commandment is understood as referring to the inalienable right of an individual not to have his or her property unlawfully removed, there is no contention. But what if, as a public word, it is applied to the way in which third world economies are milked dry by the express design of Europe and America demanding two dollars return for every dollar loaned?

And what does it say to the privatized utilities, anxious to diminish the wage-packets of long-serving employees in order to increase profit for recent shareholders or guarantee a salary in excess of £¼m for the chief executives?

'Oh . . . oh . . . oh . . .' I hear someone objecting. 'You can't take the Ten Commandments and begin to apply them willy-nilly to political and commercial life today. They were written in a pre-literate, non-European society.'

By the same token, you can't take them and apply them to private

behaviour and personal morality today. They were written in an era
when such considerations were secondary.

Perhaps I sympathize with a former Prime Minister who said that he
usually left morality to the churches, but in later life felt he had to
deliberate on it himself. For if the churches begin to take these gracious words of God not as the individualistic advice notes of a private
chaplain to his fawning admirers, but as the public statements of the
Lord of All addressed to the nations and societies of earth, then the
churches' pronouncements on morality will be much more all-perva-
sive and poignant.

As long as we argue with each other about when a fertilized egg becomes a human being in order to inform the abortion debate, no one
will be terror struck. But if instead we allow *'Thou shalt not kill'* to
inform our deliberations about the efficacy of making purchases from
companies or giving loans to countries which encourage child labour
and its concomitant high mortality rate, then we will be labelled
offensive.

As long as we see *'Thou shalt not covet'* as a gentle and quaint admoni-
tion against keeping up with the Joneses, Christians will fulfil their
harmless sitcom stereotype. But if such a gracious word leads us to
question the right of highly profitably industries to create, through
advertising, an unnatural thirst or lust for their product, particularly
among those who cannot afford it, we will enter far more disputed
waters.

Three years ago in a Roman Catholic parish in Chicago, the priest
and several parishioners were summoned to court to answer charges
of defamation and malicious damage brought against them by a large
brewery. This establishment had recently produced a new beer with
an unusually high alcohol content. Knowing that in the area of the
city which included St Barbara's parish there was a high rate of un-

employment, and therefore a high rate of casual drinking and alco-
holism, the brewers took over prime poster sites to advertise their
product.

The local Catholic church, aware that the sure consequence of this
allurement to men who were vulnerable would be that even more of
their social security money went into the pub tills and even less to
their wives and children, decided to take action. The priest and some
members took paint and defaced the expensive hoarding posters. Hence
the prosecution.

When in court, the priest and his parishioners made it clear that they
could not, in all conscience, allow the vulnerable to be put into a situation where they were forced to covet what they couldn't afford. In due
course they attracted such local and national publicity that not only
was the case dropped, but the brewery discontinued its new line.

Take each of the Ten Commandments in turn and read them not as
petty legislation for private individuals but as the gracious response
of a God who hears the cries of the vulnerable. Seen in this way, they
become not mechanisms of social control, but words of hope and
liberation.

And if such a way of looking at the commandments is a mind-boggling
u-turn for us, then we are in good company. We are not the first to have
been so upset. For is not this what lies behind and beneath Paul's
words in the third chapter of Philippians?

There he indicates how he kept this law and that law, and lived out a
life of precise personal adherence to the counsels of perfection decreed,
it seemed, by an exacting heavenly tormentor he called God. And all
that did was to breed in him a sad concoction of self-righteousness,
censoriousness and downright hatred of people who were different.

Then, one day, he discovered that God was not law, but that God was love, and he stopped doing this and not doing that out of fear of a celestial sadist, and started living positively and fondly out of love for one who hears the cries of the poor and responds.

God did not hate the world so much that he overruled it. God loved the world so much that he came in person to save it.

Our lawgiver is first and always our lover.

9   The Renaming of God

Readings: Genesis 17.1–8; 1 Peter 2.5–10; Luke 13.10–17

> *Here is this woman . . . a daughter*
> *of Abraham.*
>
> LUKE 13.16

I don't always follow the practice of offering a title for a sermon. It can sometimes lead to confusion . . . which may be what some people are experiencing as they conjecture what is intended by the title *The renaming of God.*

'Is this some new-age perversion?' someone might ask. 'Has he been set up by the feminists to tell us about Sophia instead of the Saviour?'

Listening to all the passages of scripture read earlier you might have recognized that the title has less to do with the renaming of *God*, than it has with the *renaming* of God. It alludes to the fond habit in the heart of the Almighty for changing the nomenclature of the servants of God.

RENAMING THE ANCIENTS

We saw it first in the story of Abram, the old man, the pensioner, the senior citizen, the nonagenarian, one year off a hundred. Abram – as spelt – meant 'High or Great Father' which might have been nothing more than a term of endearment. In a similar way, single women in Holland who have reached years of seniority are called Mevrouw (the equivalent of Mrs) even though they have never married or borne children.

It was that kind of honorary title which was bestowed on Abram, the old man, grandfather, though truth to tell he had not sired any prog-

States of **BLISS** & *yearning*

eny from his almost as ancient wife.

But in the fullness of time God determines that this is the man he wants to be the progenitor of the Jewish nation, the chosen people. And so, in the light of God's promise and expectation, Abram is *renamed* Abraham. The 'High Father' becomes the 'Father of Many'.

Later in the book of Genesis, we find how Abram's wife was also renamed by God. She had originally been called Sarai, a name that means 'Mockery', because that had been her lot in life. Having borne no children, she would have been commonly considered to be a mockery to her husband.

But God needs more than a man to start a nation, so this old lady, this mocked woman, has a name change. Sarai becomes Sarah. The one who was called Miss Mockery becomes Princess.

Isn't that tremendous!

Who else would tell a ninety-year-old woman that she was going to become pregnant? Who else would dare call a woman of that age and of that pedigree Princess?

Only God . . .

Only God . . . who gives barren people new names which point not to the disappointment in them, but to their potential.

RENAMING THE NOBODIES

The second reading, from the first letter of Peter, includes verses alluding to the experience of those who were the first Christians. We do not know their individual names. But we do know that collectively they had, at least in their own estimation and probably in the estimation of the Jews, no significance.

80

They were a collection of recently converted pagans who had nothing in common with Jesus as regards race or language. They had no proud religious pedigree. They could not, like the converted Jews, claim a historical role in seeing the Messianic promise fulfilled. They were nothings and nobodies, and they knew it.

But God knew more than they did. God knew that salvation was not for some religious elite. God knew that discipleship was determined not by race but by grace. So God *renamed* these nothings and nobodies.

Can we imagine what it must have felt like to be gathered for worship in a first-century church, perhaps hiding from persecutors, and feeling unsure of your identity, and then hearing Peter's letter to you read aloud:

> *You . . . you are a chosen race,*
> *you . . . are a royal priesthood,*
> *you . . . are a dedicated nation,*
> *you . . . are a people claimed by God for his own.*
> *Once you were not a people;*
> *now you are God's people.*

Who else would invest with supreme value those who felt they had no worth?

Who else would call unsophisticated, unordained folk 'royal priests'?

Only God . . .

Only God . . . who has chosen those who are weak, powerless and misunderstood to be trophies of grace.

RENAMING THE REJECT

So we come to the third story of God's *renaming*. It is a story with which many of us might be able to identify, but not necessarily on the side of the woman who was healed. The woman suffered from a double curse. She was physically deformed. The Gospel records:

> *She was possessed of a spirit which had crippled her for eighteen years. She was bent double and quite unable to stand up straight.* (Luke 13.11)

And bad as that was, bad as the physical deformity was, she suffered from what many similarly deformed and disabled people endure – not just the pain but the *stigma* of being visibly different.

A woman like this might have been called a hunchback. Having heard that word from adults, children might have shouted it at her in the street, knowing she couldn't run after them. Children are not all innocence. Or perhaps adults would tell their kids to keep back from her, and they would pretend she was a witch. Or naively associating physical deformity with mental malfunction, adults and children might have called her a lunatic – 'Mad Margaret' or something of that sort.

We sometimes demonize difficult people, don't we? And didn't they also do that in Jesus' day, with their talk of spirits and possession?

So when Christ meets this woman, there is a double cure for the double curse. Firstly, her disfigurement is eradicated. He lets her walk tall.

But Christ knows that that is not enough, for while she has been physically transformed, the old names, the old stigma, will stick. So, to the astonishment of his critics and her accusers, he stands beside her in the middle of the synagogue and he gives her a new name.

She was the cripple, the hunchback, the lunatic, Mad Margaret.

But now . . .

> *Here is this woman, a daughter of Abraham.*

And while we might not fully understand the significance of his words, we can sense their importance.

A moment ago she was shunned, outcast, presumed to be mad. She was not 'one of us'. She was different. She had to be avoided.

And now, as all eyes turn towards her, a new name is given. She is a *daughter of Abraham*. She is a child of the living God. She is made in God's image. She is destined for God's love.

Who else would call the very one whose appearance all despised a daughter of Abraham, a child of the living God?

Only Jesus . . .

Only Jesus . . . who sees beyond what others notice, to the beauty within that is more than skin deep.

RENAMING OURSELVES

This renaming, so beloved of God, is a holy ministry to which the Church and its members are called. For all of us have a 'past' and all of us have problems, and all of us can live under the cloud of who or what we have been, and what is up with us now.

One of the less savoury aspects of contemporary society seems to be the desire to categorize people according to their deficiencies, rather than call them by their names.

So we talk about the physically challenged, the mentally challenged, the abuse victim, the anorexic, the overeater, the divorcee, the single parent, the cross-dresser, the agoraphobic.

And true as these descriptions might be, there are two greater truths with which we have to deal in the face of Jesus Christ.

The one is that God does not define us by our problems or our past.

And if God does not, why should we?

There is a phrase which has crept into common currency in many churches, a good phrase as originally used by a Roman Catholic theologian. It is the phrase *wounded healer*. It echoes the thought of Dietrich Bonhoeffer that *'only a suffering God can help'*. In order to be the means of restoration, Christ makes himself vulnerable, wounded, at one with humanity, and out of pain and rejection completes the work of salvation.

Applied to Christians, it can suggest that those best able to help others are people who are aware of their own weaknesses.

I would fully endorse the efficacy of this kind of solidarity as a means to recovery. But sometimes those who see themselves as wounded healers spend more time talking about their wounds and encouraging voyeurism than enabling the healing process to begin.

God does not define us by our problems or our past. Nor should we. There are times when Jane, the overweight single mother, has to leave the baggage behind and be plain Jane. There are times when Robert, the abused ex-con, has to let his past be past and simply be Robert.

The bent-double woman whom Jesus healed would never have been completely cured as long as she was diminished by the stigma which had been attached to her. She had both to walk tall and to believe that her prime identity was that of a daughter of Abraham, a beautiful child of God.

Are you prepared to walk as one whose main description is a beautiful child of God – or are you going to hang on to the other names you call yourself or others call you?

God does not define us by our problems.

RENAMING OTHERS

Secondly, in the light of this miracle, we have to make some decisions about how we may be involved in the holy ministry of renaming not just ourselves but others. Let me testify to the efficacy of such a pursuit.

One of my obsessions in life is persuading people that they can sing. One in four of adults believe they can't sing, simply because at a vulnerable time in their lives someone – a parent, friend or teacher – told them they couldn't. And they live under the shadow of that pronouncement. They sometimes even give themselves a title – the groaner, the crow, the drone.

I don't believe that God would ask us to sing him a new song unless he knew it was possible. So I try to persuade people to forget what was said to them in the past, and believe that they have the voice of an apprentice angel.

I was teaching a course one weekend in Edinburgh. To this came some people from one of the most deprived public housing areas in Europe. Among them was a woman called Rose who challenged my assumption that everyone can sing because she had a voice like a corncrake in the off-season.

However, I persevered. We sang a whole lot of different kinds of music that weekend, including chants from the Russian Orthodox Church. Nothing would have even vaguely corresponded to Rose's usual musical tastes, which were firmly Country and Western.

I was astounded to get a phone call from her two weeks later, asking if I would come on a Friday evening to the church where she worshipped in order to help a group of marginalized people to pray. I arrived in this most desperate of areas and was taken into a room full of people whose faces and demeanour told a thousand stories. Several were recovering alcoholics; some were recently out of prison; some were parents whose children had been removed from them by the courts.

I was reeling internally, wondering how on earth to begin, when Rose said: 'There'll be no difficulty with the singing. I told them two weeks ago that I was an apprentice angel and that if I could sing, so could they. We can all do the *Kyrie Eleison*.'

So, in that direst of neighbourhoods, and in the dingiest of church halls, we lit a candle and dimmed the room lights, and I invited people as they wished to speak to Jesus about what was on their hearts as if he were sitting next to them. And after each prayer, after each deep heart-wrung and heart-rending prayer, this fragile company of noth- ings and nobodies sang a Russian Orthodox *Kyrie*, 'Lord have mercy', with abject devotion, thanks to a wee woman with a voice like a corncrake who believed she was an apprentice angel.

I don't imagine that this side of time I will ever again be privileged to share in prayer which was as close to heaven, and to join in singing which had the integrity of an angelic choir.

You see this woman . . . she is a daughter of Abraham.

You see this man . . . he is a son of Abraham.

You see yourselves . . . you are children of the living God.

That is your name.

That is your true identity.

Live up to it.

10 Five Missing Women

Readings: Exodus 2.23 – 3.20; St John 6.24–40

Between Matins and Evensong in this Abbey today, there have been four hours and five missing women.

Not just five *missing* women, but five perfidious women, five defiant women, five conspiratorial women.

And I will name them: Shiphrah, Puah, Jochebed, Miriam and Bithiah.

It may sound as if I'm alluding to a misguided group of female Middle-Eastern terrorists, lost somewhere in the Abbey.

But these five perfidious, defiant, conspiratorial women who have gone missing in the past four hours are not Middle-Eastern terrorists – at least, not of the present-day variety.

They are all dead and, worse than that, their stories have been excised from public view.

Let me explain the conundrum.

THE MISSING LECTION

In the Anglican Communion, the Old Testament readings for Morning Prayer and Evensong follow in sequence. At the moment, they are taking up the story of the Exodus in which Moses prefigures Jesus as the saviour of his people.

At Matins today, the Lectionary, or reading plan, prescribed a passage from the beginning of the book of Exodus concerning the state of subjugation under which the Hebrews in Egypt laboured. This evening we read the story of Moses being called by God at the burning bush.

What lies in-between is every bit as important. Indeed if what lies in-between had not happened, there would most certainly have been no Moses. The intervening narrative involves five women.

The first two, Shiphrah and Puah, were midwives who defied the government in order to save life. The Pharaoh of the day, in order to diminish the threat of the foreign workforce, ordered the Hebrew midwives to kill any male child at birth. Years after this decree, the Pharaoh, who was not blind, noticed there were still distinctly Jewish-looking boys in the streets. He asked Shiphrah and Puah why this was, and with unique female ingenuity they said, 'Your majesty, Jewish women are built differently from Egyptian women. The Egyptians go into labour for hours, but with the Jews, it's two contractions, a quick shove, and little Moshe appears in the world before we've rung the doorbell' – or words to that effect.

They defied male authority, male governmental authority, in order to save lives.

The other three women were their co-conspirators. They are not named in the Bible, but in the Talmud, an ancient Jewish commentary. Jochebed was a Hebrew woman who gave birth to a son and, with her daughter, defied the ruling power by putting the baby into a tarred basket and pushing it into the river before the proponents of infanticide could slaughter the innocent.

And, most unlikely of all, Bithiah was one of Pharaoh's daughters who spotted the baby in the basket, recognized that it was a Hebrew boy and, in defiance of her own father, adopted it for her own. She asked Miriam, the boy's sister, whom she spotted on the river bank, to find a nurse to rear the child, presumably with royal protection. This child was Moses, chronologically the first deliverer of the Jewish people. And his birth and early years were made possible by five women who conspired together to defy governmental authority, so that life could be preserved.

WHY THE SIN OF OMISSION?

What a magnificent story of heroic compassion. Yet many churches in different parts of the world would never bother to read it in public. Why is this?

Is it because those who decide what scriptures will be read in our churches do not think it is an important part of the Judaeo-Christian tradition? Or is it because the story involves women who – rather than be the chattels of their husbands, rather than be the normal run-of-the-mill biblical wife, harlot or concubine, rather than obey male authority without question – act instead with selfless humanity?

Or is it because that story shows up men in a bad light. I mean, what were all the Hebrew men doing when midwives were being told to slaughter boys at birth? Where was the macho paternal instinct then?

Or is it, perhaps, that here are five women who together conspire to exercise personal and political power, and that's not something that men, whether they be enslaved Hebrew males, or Anglican lectionary editors, or run-of-the-mill white Anglo-Saxon males find it easy to cope with?

TROUBLE FOR MEN

At this, some people may be getting hot under the clerical collar.

Perhaps someone wants to say, 'Has no one told this bearded Presbyterian idiot that the Church of England now ordains women? The battle's over. No need to bring in foot soldiers from the north!'

My own denomination has ordained women for almost twenty years. Now we see that that battle is but a diversion, a skirmish, compared to the far bigger task of empowering women in the Church by allowing their aspirations, their insights, their defiance, their passions, to be put fully at the service of the Gospel.

I was working recently for the Roman Catholic Church in Australia, and was present at a series of National Liturgical Music Conventions where, of course, the principal speakers were men. Wisely, however, the organizers had ensured that after every priestly presentation, there would be a response by a laywoman.

In Melbourne one of the responses was given by Dr Muriel Porter, an Anglican journalist and church historian. She began by taking issue with the presumption of the male speaker that the Church now had to attend to its liturgy more than ever before, because that was the place where most believers gathered. She commented that in a day when church attendances were dropping, it was perhaps more important to look to the people rather than to the liturgy.

She continued:

> *The common presumption is that fewer men are coming to*
> *church today. The reality is, and research bears this out, that*
> *fewer women are going to church. Men have never gone. The*
> *women have always had to drag them and the children as*
> *well. And now, when women have more self-confidence, but*
> *are still marginalized in the decision-making processes of the*
> *church locally or nationally, they vote with their feet.*

As she spoke, I noticed some women near me in tears, and others biting hard on their handkerchiefs to keep themselves from whooping in disbelief that what they knew to be true was at last being articulated.

But this truth is not something peculiar to the mainline Western traditions of Christianity.

A friend of mine, Milos Vesin, a priest in the Serbian Orthodox Church, surprised me when I asked him how he – in a very patriarchal tradition – viewed the place of women.

He said, 'It is only now that we are beginning to value the importance and the gift of women in our church. Now we can reflect on the days of communist oppression when seminaries were shut, churches were turned into warehouses and there was no religious instruction of children.'

'Then,' he said '. . . then it was the mothers and grandmothers who, while feeding, washing and bedding the children, would *subversively* tell them the stories of the faith in order that future generations might believe.'

REMEMBER THE WOMEN

Remember Shiphrah,

remember Puah,

remember Jochebed,

remember Miriam,

remember Bithiah,

. . . for their suppressed stories of courage and defiance may perhaps be mirrored in a thousand parishes today where the real heroes of the faith are unsung heroines.

Remember them, you who are women, and take courage from their courage.

Remember them, you who are men, because yours is the gender which has, in humility, to change the systems of power, language, decision-making and association which continue to marginalize women.

Remember them, because they prefigure in their defiance that girl without whose subversive canticle, the Magnificat, no Evensong would be complete.

Remember them, especially Shiphrah and Puah, because they share the profession of midwife with God who, when the waters break, delivers her people.

11 Table Talk

Readings: Revelation 19.5–10; St Luke 11.37–45 & 53–54

> *Did he who made the outside*
> *not make the inside too?*
> LUKE 11 V 40

When I grew up in Kilmarnock in the sixties, there were three realities which people referred to in muted tones.

I will say the words loudly: CANCER, CATHOLICS and WOMEN'S TROUBLE.

One would be listening to a conversation in which someone's name was mentioned, and suddenly a voice would interject, 'Oh she's a nice woman Mrs Darroch. But did you know? She's got (*whisper*).'

Not hearing what was being said about Mrs Darroch one could still guarantee that she either had cancer, had discovered some kind of gynaecological irregularity, or attended St Joseph's.

This was the way in which Mrs Dunlop spoke. I knew her. She was a widow, and her granddaughter had gone to school with me. Frequently on a Sunday at lunchtime the extended Dunlop family – two sons and their wives and their children – would descend on Brodick Crescent where Mrs Dunlop would preside over the meal table and monitor every conversation.

AN AWKWARD LUNCH

But on this particular Sunday things were rather tricky. On this particular Sunday Alec, Mrs Dunlop's oldest grandson, was coming with his fiancee.

He had been going out with the girl for two years, and had been engaged to her for six months, but had not yet dared to introduce her to his grandmother because her name was Theresa. She was a (*Catholic*)! And Mrs Dunlop was one of those believers whose identity came both from loving the Lord and from thanking God that she was a Protestant.

So, very gingerly, Alec brought Theresa into his grandmother's house. The rest of the family – his parents, his aunt and uncle, his brothers and sisters and cousins – all made sure that Mrs Dunlop was engaged in conversation that never touched on anything vaguely religious.

And all went relatively well until, in the middle of eating a rather indigestible baked rice pudding and when everyone's mouth was full, Mrs Dunlop ventured the comment, apropos of nothing, '*Well, there's one thing I've always said about Catholics. They're good singers!*'

You can imagine the embarrassment which made the family almost regurgitate the indigestible dessert. Even if it was the right word, it was certainly the wrong time, and the family did not leave that meal table with a good taste in their mouth.

How like Jesus was Mrs Dunlop. How like Jesus!

That's not a question, it's a statement. I say that because all the evidence – and I mean *all* the evidence – we have about Jesus at meal tables is that he inevitably said the right thing at the wrong time. At the very least he caused upset; and at best he created livid consternation. (And to think that some of us refer to him as the passive 'unseen guest at every table'.)

JESUS' TABLE MANNERS

I stake my claim particularly on the record of our Lord's behaviour which is provided by Luke's Gospel.

Some scholars view Luke's Gospel as a compendium of meals and journeys with Jesus. And that description is not far from the truth. For he does wander about a lot. And he does eat a lot.

Indeed, in Luke's Gospel we see Jesus at a meal table on ten different occasions, and on no one occasion is the table talk without an element of surprise.

We find him in Levi's house, where the society watchers complain that he is sitting down to eat with tax-gatherers and sinners. And he insults his critics by saying that perhaps they need his company more than those who are pickled in self-righteousness.

He dines in the house of Simon the leper and disgusts his host not only by allowing a woman to wash his feet with her tears, but by telling Simon that the woman is showing him up when it comes to real hospitality.

He upsets Martha, the industrious housewife, by telling her to stop fussing about whether there's enough gravy in the stew, and instead sit down and listen to him.

He confounds the disciples in an upstairs room when, in the middle of a fellowship meal, he says that one of the company is going to betray him.

There are ten occasions recorded in the gospel when Jesus is at a meal table and the conversation in every case is far from dull.

This is never more so than on the occasion when Jesus goes for lunch, for a midday meal, to the house of a distinguished Pharisee. Before long, his host notices that Jesus has not followed the correct etiquette. He has not washed his hands before eating. This 'Son of God' is in breach of godly procedure.

So the Pharisee takes him to task by asking him if he isn't going to wash his hands first. And what does Jesus do? Say, 'It doesn't matter.'?

> *You Pharisees clean the outside of the cup and plate. But*
> *inside you are full of greed and wickedness. You fools! Did he*
> *who made the outside not make the inside too?*

Can you imagine the silence that would follow that outburst? Mrs Dunlop has nothing on Jesus when it comes to saying the right thing at the wrong time.

But he has not finished. Some sensitive souls who have come to this meal are lawyers; and they feel that they are being got at by Jesus' comments. So one of them says to him,

'Teacher, when you say things like this, you are insulting us too.'

And what does Jesus say? . . . 'I'm sorry, I wasn't referring to you. I was speaking to the holy rollers.'?

Not a bit of it.

> *Alas for you lawyers too! You load men with intolerable*
> *burdens, and you will not lift a finger to lighten the load.*

At least Mrs Dunlop normally kept her voice down when referring to what she considered unsavoury. Jesus roars it out for all to hear. You can't imagine the Rotary Club of the day, having learned of his tendencies, inviting him to come as an after-dinner speaker.

Having torn strips off the Pharisees, having exposed the hypocrisy of the lawyers, what might he say to the bankers or accountants to give them a red face? What might he say to the shopkeepers and small businessmen who come for meat and two veg and a harmless homily peppered with courteous humour?

When Jesus Christ is about, the borderline between a business lunch and a barney is hard to detect.

No wonder some of the more liberal commentators want to suggest that probably this never happened when Christ came to the Pharisee's table. Luke, they say, just invented a location for these penetrating words of Jesus.

I disdain such suggestions, for there are another nine instances in the gospel where meals taken in the presence of Jesus are a blessing to some and a provocation to others.

What are we to make of it – we who are about to sit round a table hosted by this same provocative Jesus?

INSIDE AND OUTSIDE

I want to look particularly at the words of Jesus to his host which, whether spoken loudly in anger or quietly in a whisper, convey deep pathos:

Did he who made the outside not make the inside too?

Here, Jesus is at his penetratingly simplest and best. For in the face of these paragons of propriety, these exemplars of religious behaviour, he exposes the fraudulence of their existence which no one else had noticed, namely that all this show, all this obsession with detail, all this prissiness about what was right, was a cover-up for lives of interior inadequacy.

Here is Jesus exposing that behind the flawless facade of those who would be society's role models were individuals who identified what was wrong in others to prevent others recognizing what was wrong in them.

Did he who made the outside not make the inside too?

And perhaps, in our more honest moments, we who do not claim to be

Pharisees recognize that these words speak deeply to our experience. For have we not noticed, have we not seen, how some of the people who most extol the virtue of family values are people whose own marriages are perilously shaky. Some of the people who make the loudest noises about the need to enforce law and order are people whose own business practices leave much to be desired. Some of the people who protest loudest about the need to pray and read the Scriptures and be converted are folk in whose lives the spiritual gifts of humility, sensitivity and forgiveness are singularly lacking.

Haven't you noticed, friends of Jesus Christ, that we are all at our most self-righteous when we have something to hide?

Did he who made the outside not make the inside too?

This penetrating and, to some, insulting word of Jesus is an antidote to the kind of breakdowns which are all too common in the busy lives of people today.

What is a breakdown? Doctors and psychologists will use differing terminology to describe it, but apparent to all is the simple truth that a breakdown happens when there is an unhealthy distance between the outer person and the inner person.

The outer man is busy on a thousand fronts, the inner man is having no time spent on him. The outer woman is putting the world to rights, the inner woman has serious troubles which are being overlooked. The outer self is gregariously entertaining everyone, and inside there is a child crouching in a corner waiting to be loved.

But Jesus Christ is not impressed by the outward display, whether it be of piety or righteousness or good manners or perfect procedure, if that is at odds with an inner self which is emaciated, damaged or denied.

And what is the cure for all this? What is the medicine for the soul?

What is the remedy for the inside which God also made?

When we come to sit round the Lord's table, we are not offered an elaborate meal to threaten our waistline. This is not a five-star restaurant.

We are offered a fragment of bread and a sip of wine through which Jesus Christ in his fullness enters our inside to deal with the dirt, the frustration, the yearning, which our external lives disguise.

God, who made the outside, made the inside too, and in this sacrament God provides a specific moment and a specific means whereby, depending on him, we can be healed, forgiven, blessed and made new again.

It is not your stomach which Christ is entering, it is your soul.

Will you make a place for him?

12 The Lawbreaker and the Evangelist

Readings: Genesis 24.15–28; St John 4.5–26

> *Jesus said to the Samaritan*
> *woman, 'Give me a drink'*
> *(JOHN 4 V 7)*

I don't know what you make of this story of Jesus with the woman at the well. But recently my understanding of it has radically changed.

I used to believe that the only important thing about the story was Jesus' often-repeated statement, *'The hour is coming when the true worshippers shall worship the Father in Spirit and in Truth.'*

But I now realize that there is much more in this encounter, partly because for the past year or more I have been reading John's Gospel a verse a day. And in so doing I have begun to realize why this gospel more than any other was beloved by the Celts, whose expression of faith has been known in Scotland for over fifteen hundred years.

John's Gospel begins with the affirmation that *the Word became flesh,* and the rest of the gospel takes great pains to point out just how much the word became flesh, how easily and closely identified with raw humanity Jesus was.

Perhaps more than any of the other gospels, it spells out with eye-witness clarity and enthusiasm the very human encounters Jesus had with people, in the midst of which he revealed the most profound truths about the love of God and the purpose of his own mission.

It has been my engagement with people in one of the poorest parishes in Glasgow that has helped me, at the same time, to recognize that the people with whom Jesus interacts in the gospel are indeed flesh and blood people – not stained-glass window people, nor King James Version of the Bible people, but folk who can be as remarkably candid, earthy and at times irreverent as any of their present day equivalents.

What I want to suggest (though, goodness knows, some people might find it upsetting) is that this story of the encounter of Jesus with a woman at the well is actually quite a salacious little tale.

A SAUCY STORY?

I am not for a moment suggesting that it might provide copy fit for the tabloids, but I do believe that the story is peppered with allusion and innuendo which only become apparent when we begin to envisage the scene and hear the dialogue with real rather than religious imagination.

Let us remember that this story of a man and a woman at a well is not the only such in the Bible. There was another well where a servant of Abraham stopped and asked for a drink. This was the means of locating a wife-to-be of Abraham's son, Isaac. And though this is not alluded to in John's account, it was there in the Jewish folk memory of anyone who saw or heard what was going on.

Let us also remember that the disciples were astonished when they came back to Jesus and discovered him in conversation with this unknown woman. So, with a feeling for the possible irregularity of the encounter, let us go through the story again and allow ourselves the odd aside.

Jesus goes to a well at midday.

A woman comes to draw water.

> (. . . Midday is a funny time to draw water.
> You do that in the morning when the sun

is not so hot.)

He says, 'Give me a drink.'

(. . . How does she, who is a bit of a
trollop, take this request? As an indication of thirst, or as a chat-up line to get
the conversation going?)

She expresses surprise that, as a Jew, he is asking a Samaritan for
a drink.

(. . . Does this not confirm her curiosity as
to what he is after, given that Jews and
Samaritans do not share drinking vessels?)

He says that if she knew who he was, she would ask him to give her
water.

(. . . And in what exactly was he going to
contain it?)

He says the water he gives, unlike the water in the well, is everlasting.

(. . . What does that mean? Perhaps she
thinks that if she can get some, it will prevent her becoming bow-legged through end-
lessly carrying buckets to the well. So she
asks for some of this 'special' water.)

He tells her to go and call her husband.

(. . . Why? Is this a ploy to find out if she
has a husband?)

She says she doesn't have a husband.

*(. . . Is this a declaration that she is
'available'?)*

And then . . . and only then, when he says, *'You're right you don't have a husband!'*, only then does she realize that the dusky stranger is more than a potential suitor. And the conversation which ensues is one that changes her whole life.

To those who have heard the story many times before, it seems like a pious conversation between a penitent sinner and Jesus. But as seen and heard through the eyes and ears of a neutral observer, this encounter has all the overtones of a potential romance. In this curious story, there are three transformations that take place, each of which is worthy of our attention.

LORD TO LAWBREAKER

The first is that the Lord becomes a lawbreaker.

This is exactly what Jesus does, and he knows it.

Jewish etiquette dictated three rules of thumb or, more accurately, rules of engagement which Jesus deliberately broke.

1. Jewish men did not talk to unknown women in the open. Women were chattels, secondary citizens, beneath pitying, as illustrated by the fervent prayer, 'I thank you O God that you did not make me a woman.'

So for a Jewish man to be seen in a situation of dependence on a woman, asking for a drink in a public place, was to break rule number one.

2. A Jewish rabbi, even more than a Jewish layman, would never get himself into the position of being liable to public ridicule for doing something forbidden. And what was expressly forbidden was a friendly conversation with a Samaritan. It would be as incongruous as Gerry Adams asking Baroness Thatcher to join him for a drink at the Athenaeum.

3. Samaritans being beneath the contempt of Jews, no self-respecting Jew would ever use the same eating utensils or drinking vessels. Unless they had been ritually purified, their use would ensure instant contamination. Here we have the Lord of Hosts, the King of Glory, the Prince of Peace, the Messiah, the fulfilment of the hopes of his people, visibly infringing the rules by which his people lived, running the risk of public defamation and threatening to bring his own tradition into disrepute.

This is the Lord whom we worship, this is the Christ to whom we sing, to whom we pray, behind whom we follow. And he is a lawbreaker.

The story illustrates how Christ defies the petty regulations which we often carefully observe in order to keep ourselves on the right side of God. Conventional respectability may be important when it comes to deciding pecking order at the Lord Mayor's Banquet or the Hunt Ball. Social etiquette has its purpose in ensuring that wedding receptions do not turn into brawls and that formal occasions do not descend into the anarchy of a jumble sale.

But we have a Lord who, when the situation requires it, breaks the rules, disregards the conventions, lets us down in our expectation of how God should behave. And he does this because those who are lost, those who are on the periphery, those who would never come near the church, are infinitely precious in his sight. Sometimes therefore we shall have to forgo our prissiness in order fully to represent our Saviour.

TROLLOP TO EVANGELIST

The second transformation is that the woman, the trollop, becomes an evangelist.

When I asked my friends in a Glasgow parish to suggest what this woman might have looked like, they thought she would be in her early forties, smoke a lot, have dyed red hair, wear cheap lipstick and dangly earrings and be busty in appearance and cheeky in speech.

I don't know if you have ever met a woman who has seen off five husbands and is staying with her current live-in lover, but I hardly imagine that she would be the type to appear on the front cover of *Homes and Gardens* or *The People's Friend*.

Maybe she was a woman whose face told the story of a cheapened life and brutal treatment at the hands of her suitors. Maybe from her school days she had been known as an easy lay and had never known the tenderness or the respect she deserved. Maybe she had seen the way that her father had treated her mother and expected, as some women do, to be beaten and abused in the same way.

Is this too extreme a suggestion? Then remember that it was recently reported that a woman is beaten in the USA every fifteen seconds. And if in Britain the frequency is less, it will be only because we have a smaller population, not because we are a morally superior nation.

Maybe she was just hoping that in this stranger at the well she might find the kind of man who would treat her with the kind of dignity no other man had shown.

And indeed this happened, but not because she was swept off her feet and engaged in some gentle but illicit sex. Rather it was because this man who knew all about her did not want to assault her or use her for his own pleasure. His delight was in allowing her to know that whoever she was and whatever she had been, she was a child of God and deserving of the best.

This man persuaded her that if she allowed her deepest yearnings for self-respect, for acceptance, for a sense of belonging, to be directed to the love of God, then she would indeed be able to discover her true worth.

The profound declaration of Jesus' interest in her life is such that during the course of the ambiguous conversation, she changes. She is transformed from a worthless trollop to an enthusiastic evangelist. For after she has spoken with this man, she goes to tell the whole village, whose inhabitants come to find him.

I cannot understand how people who are opposed to the ordination of women deal with this text. For here, as in many other stories in the Scriptures, it is a woman or women who are explicitly the bearers, the bringers, the tellers of Good News.

So we see Jesus transformed from Lord to Lawbreaker, and we see the woman transformed from trollop to evangelist.

And all through the story another transformation is running – what begins as a conversation ends as a conversion.

CONVERSATION TO CONVERSION

Here we see the genius of Jesus Christ whose desire is to enter into a relationship of mutuality with all whom he calls. Note that the first thing he does is ask the woman to do something which she can do. And in the conversation that follows, she embarks on a relationship which develops beyond her wildest dreams.

At first she just thinks she is talking to an-off duty rabbi with an eye for gentile women, and gradually she realizes that she is speaking to the Son of God who has asked her to do something for him.

He did not begin his encounter by saying: *'I have come that you might have eternal life.'* If he had, she would have run a mile.

He did not begin by saying: *'Would you like to know about an untapped spiritual reservoir?'* If he had, she would have dismissed him as a crank.

His method of evangelism, if we can call it that, is to engage people in doing what they can and not force them to grapple with what is beyond them.

It is the same with Peter, Andrew, James and John. Jesus does not ask them if they would like to become apostles. He asks them, whose trade is fishing, to use their skill in a new direction.

It is the same with the rich young man. He does not ask him if he would like to become ordained as a mark of discipleship. The youth's language is the language of money. So Jesus asks him to give some of it away.

I used to be puzzled when I was asked to speak at church conferences about being a Christian from Monday to Saturday. I did not understand why such an issue should be in people's minds.

But gradually I realized that the model for discipleship which the church has too often held up to laypeople is that of a priest, monk or minister, as if ordination were the goal of Christian endeavour. What nonsense!

Jesus Christ never asked those who met him to become a rabbi like himself. He always asked them to do what they could for him, even when it was a simple request like, 'Give me a drink.'

For it is when we use the potentials God has given us to advance the purposes of his kingdom that we become partners with, rather than strangers to, our Lord.

I do not know you. I do not know your potentials. I do not know what for you would be the equivalent of Jesus Christ asking the woman at the well for a drink.

But I do know that when you give to God and do for God whatever you can, you move from the fringe to the centre, from isolation to belonging, from doubt to understanding, from conversation to conversion.

The Iona Community

The Iona Community is an ecumenical Christian community, founded in 1938 by the late Lord MacLeod of Fuinary (the Revd George MacLeod DD) and committed to seeking new ways of living the Gospel in today's world. Gathered around the rebuilding of the ancient monastic buildings of Iona Abbey, but with its original inspiration in the poorest areas of Glasgow during the Depression, the Community has sought ever since the 'rebuilding of the common life', bringing together work and worship, prayer and politics, the sacred and the secular in ways that reflect its strongly incarnational theology.

The Community today is a movement of some 200 Members, over 1,400 Associate Members and about 1,600 Friends. The Members — women and men from many backgrounds and denominations, most in Britain, but some overseas — are committed to a rule of daily prayer and Bible reading, sharing and accounting for their use of time and money, regular meeting and action for justice and peace.

The Iona Community maintains three centres on Iona and Mull: Iona Abbey and the MacLeod Centre on Iona, and Camas Adventure Camp on the Ross of Mull. Its base is in Community House, Glasgow, where it also supports work with young people, the Wild Goose Resource and Worship Groups, a bimonthly magazine (*Coracle*) and a publishing house (Wild Goose Publications).

For further information on the Iona Community please contact:

The Iona Community
Pearce Institute,
840 Govan Road
Glasgow G51 3UU
T. 0141 445 4561; **F.** 0141 445 4295
e-mail: ionacomm@gla.iona.org.uk

Other Titles from Wild Goose Publications

SONGBOOKS with full music (titles marked * have companion cassettes)

SEVEN SONGS OF MARY*, John Bell
SEVEN PSALMS OF DAVID*, John Bell
SEVEN PSALMS OF DAVID - PACK OF OCTAVOS* John Bell
LOVE AND ANGER*, John Bell and Graham Maule
WHEN GRIEF IS RAW, John Bell and Graham Maule
THE LAST JOURNEY - PACK OF 15 OCTAVOS* John Bell
THE LAST JOURNEY reflections*, John Bell
THE COURAGE TO SAY NO: 23 SONGS FOR EASTER & LENT*J Bell & G Maule
GOD NEVER SLEEPS – PACK OF 12 OCTAVOS* John Bell
COME ALL YOU PEOPLE, Shorter Songs for Worship* John Bell
PSALMS OF PATIENCE, PROTEST AND PRAISE* John Bell
HEAVEN SHALL NOT WAIT (Wild Goose Songs Vol.1)* J Bell & Graham Maule
ENEMY OF APATHY (Wild Goose Songs Vol.2) J Bell & Graham Maule
LOVE FROM BELOW (Wild Goose Songs Vol.3)* John Bell & Graham Maule
INNKEEPERS & LIGHT SLEEPERS* (for Christmas) John Bell
MANY & GREAT (Songs of the World Church Vol.1)* John Bell (ed./arr.)
SENT BY THE LORD (Songs of the World Church Vol.2)* John Bell (ed./arr.)
FREEDOM IS COMING* Anders Nyberg (ed.)
PRAISING A MYSTERY, Brian Wren
BRING MANY NAMES, Brian Wren

CASSETTES & CDs (titles marked † have companion songbooks)

Cassette, SEVEN SONGS OF MARY/SEVEN PSALMS OF DAVID, † John Bell (guest conductor)
CD, SEVEN SONGS OF MARY/SEVEN PSALMS OF DAVID, † John Bell (guest conductor)
Cassette, LOVE AND ANGER, † Wild Goose Worship Group
CD, THE LAST JOURNEY, † John Bell (guest conductor)
Cassette, THE LAST JOURNEY, † John Bell (guest conductor)

Cassette, IONA ABBEY, WORSHIP FROM EASTER WEEK (ed/arr Steve Butler)
Cassette, THE COURAGE TO SAY NO † Wild Goose Worship Group
Cassette, GOD NEVER SLEEPS † John Bell (guest conductor)
CD, GOD NEVER SLEEPS † John Bell (guest conductor)
Cassette, COME ALL YOU PEOPLE † Wild Goose Worship Group
CD, PSALMS OF PATIENCE, PROTEST AND PRAISE † Wild Goose Worship Group
Cassette, PSALMS OF PATIENCE, PROTEST AND PRAISE † WGWG
Cassette, HEAVEN SHALL NOT WAIT † Wild Goose Worship Group
Cassette, LOVE FROM BELOW † Wild Goose Worship Group
Cassette, INNKEEPERS & LIGHT SLEEPERS † (for Christmas) WGWG
Cassette, MANY AND GREAT † Wild Goose Worship Group
Cassette, SENT BY THE LORD † Wild Goose Worship Group
Cassette, FREEDOM IS COMING † Fjedur
Cassette, TOUCHING PLACE, A, Wild Goose Worship Group
Cassette, CLOTH FOR THE CRADLE, Wild Goose Worship Group
Cassette, SIGNS OF FIRE, Ian Fraser

DRAMA BOOKS

EH JESUS...YES PETER No. 1, John Bell and Graham Maule
EH JESUS...YES PETER No. 2, John Bell and Graham Maule
EH JESUS...YES PETER No. 3, John Bell and Graham Maule

PRAYER/WORSHIP BOOKS

MEDITATIONS FROM THE IONA COMMUNITY, Ian Reid
CLOTH FOR THE CRADLE, Worship Resources and Readings for Advent, Christmas and Epiphany, Wild Goose Worship Group
THE PILGRIMS' MANUAL, Christopher Irvine
THE PATTERN OF OUR DAYS, Kathy Galloway (ed.)
PRAYERS AND IDEAS FOR HEALING SERVICES, Ian Cowie
HE WAS IN THE WORLD: Meditations for Public Worship, John Bell
EACH DAY AND EACH NIGHT: Prayers from Iona in the Celtic Tradition, Philip Newell
IONA COMMUNITY WORSHIP BOOK,
THE WHOLE EARTH SHALL CRY GLORY, George MacLeod
STRANGE FIRE, Ian Fraser

OTHER BOOKS

CHASING THE WILD GOOSE: The Story of the Iona Community, Ron Ferguson

DREAMING OF EDEN: Reflections on Christianity and Sexuality, Kathy Galloway (ed.)

THE PROSPECT OF HEAVEN: Musings of an Enquiring Believer, Frederick Levison

THE OWL AND THE STEREO, David Osborne

COLUMBA: Pilgrim and Penitent, Ian Bradley

THE EARTH UNDER THREAT: A Christian Perspective, Ghillean Prance

THE MYTH OF PROGRESS, Yvonne Burgess

WHAT IS THE IONA COMMUNITY?

PUSHING THE BOAT OUT: New Poetry, Kathy Galloway (ed.)

EXILE IN ISRAEL: A Personal Journey with the Palestinians, Runa Mackay

FALLEN TO MEDIOCRITY: CALLED TO EXCELLENCE, Erik Cramb

REINVENTING THEOLOGY AS THE PEOPLE'S WORK, Ian Fraser

STARTING WHERE WE ARE, Kathy Galloway